Staging a Musical

Matthew White

Theatre Arts Books/Routledge · New York

For Gerald and Sheila White

First published in 1999 by
A & C Black (Publishers) Limited
35 Bedford Row, London WC1R 4JH

© 1999 Matthew White

Published in the USA in 1999 by
Theatre Arts Books/Routledge
29 West 35th Street, New York, NY 10001

ISBN 0-87830-108-9

CIP catalog data is available from the Library
of Congress.

Cover photographs:
Main photograph *Carousel*, Imperial Theatre,
Tokyo, courtesy of Toho Co. Ltd
Small photographs *Into the Woods* Royal
Academy of Music, courtesy of Nik Milner

Typeset in $10^1/_2$ on 12pt Palatino
Printed in Great Britain by Biddles Ltd,
Guildford, Surrey

Contents

Acknowledgements

Special thanks to Lindsey Clay, Nick Davey, Caroline de Wolfe, Sir Cameron Mackintosh, Charlotte Sewell, Ashley Straw, Graham Wynne, also Jermyn St Theatre, Mountview Theatre School, Toho Co. Ltd, Josef Weinberger Ltd.

Thanks also to Louise Chantal, Bob Crowley, Jacqui Coghlan, Jane Elliott, Ellen Flatters, Julius Green, Theo Green, Mary Hammond, Dan Hill, Jenni Hodgson, Tesni Hollands, Sally Irwin, Liz Kaye, Emi Kazuko, Richard Mildenhall, Nick Milner, Michael Nelligan, Harriett O'Donnell, Jane Quill, Jane Roberts, Paul Sabey, Niccola Shearman, Jennifer Till

I would also like to thank the cast and production teams of the following shows; many of whom appear in the photographs featured in the book:

Carousel Akira Horigome, Shunsuke Kitamura, Shinpei Kuno, Hiroshi Miyakawa, Yoshiaki Nagahata, Eigo Shibata, Honoka Suzuki, Tetsuya Tajima

Closer Than Ever David Babani, Natasha Braithwaite, Jonathan Fensom, Charlie Fulton, Chris George, Helen Hobson, David Howe, Beverley Klein, Anne Larlarb, Martin Lowe, Mark McKerracher, Ed Morris, Gareth Snook, Phil Spencer-Hunt, Sam Spencer Lane

The Demon Headmaster Sam Kenyon, Roger Parrott, Elizabeth Renihan

Hot Mikado Gavin Ashbarry, Christopher Jefferson, Darren Morfitt, Craig Parkinson, Robert Shelley, Nick Sutcliffe

Into The Woods Stephanie Adlington, Susie Dumbreck, Loren Geeting, Gillian Kirkpatrick, Eliza Lumley, Nicola Morton, Andrea Pope, Heather Sawney, Airlie Scott

Jack The Ripper Melanie Barker, Gerard Bentall, Mirren Delaney, Sarah Hopes, Sally Hunt, Frazer Lincoln, Tim McArthur, Sarah Moffett, Natalie Ng-Yu-Tin, Todd Yard, Lesley Young

Starting Here, Starting Now Jenny Arnold, Clare Burt, Michael Cantwell, Caroline Humphris, Samantha Shaw.

Foreword

How do you produce a musical? This is a question I'm often asked and though there is no definitive answer, Matthew White has certainly set out clearly and simply the key areas of organisation that need to be addressed in order to take a project from an idea to a First Night. This is quite an achievement as staging a musical is a tremendously complex undertaking.

The dream of putting on a show must be matched by the practicality of putting all the pieces together and Matthew has expertly tracked the entire process of staging a production so that by the end of the book anyone wishing to stage a musical, whether for the amateur stage or perhaps as a future professional, will understand the complicated and wide ranging areas involved. The musical theatre is the most collaborative of arts and with any such endeavour, hand in hand with talent, must go a certain amount of ego. Having chosen the team to put on the show it is the producer's job to get the best out of everybody. Therefore, a good producer needs a combination of charm, commonsense, instinct and flair and must be able to keep cool under fire. He or she must also be good with figures and not be frightened of taking the odd calculated risk. But, above all, to have a hit you must enjoy what Alfred P. Doolittle immortally declared in *My Fair Lady*, 'a little bit of luck'.

The only thing a book like this can never tell you is how to pick successful new material: that gift has to come from within you. But if you're lucky enough to have that gift, Matthew's book certainly gives you a good insight into the huge amount of work you need to do to make your dreams come true.

Sir Cameron Mackintosh

Introduction

I was eighteen, just out of school, and living in London for the first time, when I happened to stumble across the Royal National Theatre and its uniquely entertaining production of *Guys and Dolls*. It was an experience which left an indelible impression. With its wonderful spectrum of colourful characters, the quirky wit of its script, and the sheer brilliance of its score, *Guys and Dolls* quite simply bowled me over. I suddenly understood what it meant to leave the theatre floating on air. Since then, I have seen hundreds of musicals and been involved in a wide variety of different musical theatre projects, from the small-scale fringe revue, to the multi-million-pound West End blockbuster. Every project has thrown up a whole new series of different problems, and a whole new set of challenges. This, in a nutshell, is what has made the theatre for me such an exciting, unpredictable arena.

This book examines the process of putting together a musical, from the initial impulse to the opening night and beyond. While I would be crazy to suggest that it is possible to create a step-by-step guide to the perfect musical production, I do believe that a clearer understanding of the process will better equip the prospective producer or director to face the challenges which a musical production presents. The musical, by definition, is an ambitious form of entertainment, since it relies upon a combination of disciplines – music, drama, and in many cases dance too. Casts are often larger than in the 'straight' play, costumes more elaborate, set changes more frequent, and musical accompaniment a necessity. In short, the musical is in many respects more complicated to stage than the play, and certainly brings with it a variety of problems which need to be addressed from the outset. However, it is this synthesis of music, drama and movement that can, at best, create the most exhilarating of theatrical experiences. And something which never ceases to surprise and delight me is that these experiences can happen in all sorts of different theatrical venues: in village halls; in pub theatres; in school gymnasiums; and, of course, in gorgeous old Victorian playhouses.

My observations in this book are based largely upon my own experiences as an actor and director. And the more experience that I gain, the more firmly I believe that the process of putting on a show is essentially the same whether working in an amateur or a professional environment, whether producing large-scale or small-scale work. Of course there are obvious differences – differences in size of budget, length of rehearsal time, availability of equipment and so on – but I am convinced that the same degree of commitment is required, the same standards of discipline and the same emphasis upon organisation.

Musicals come in all shapes and sizes, and there is a bewildering amount of material to choose from. This is good news for anyone wishing to put on a new production. Because of its enduring popularity, the musical has, throughout the twentieth century, twisted and turned in many directions, and there is consequently a huge selection of different works to choose from, some well-loved and constantly revived, and others more obscure and just waiting to be rediscovered. My hope in writing this book is that it will provide some guidance to those wishing to embark upon the exciting process of staging a musical, and that it will ultimately facilitate the smooth running of the whole enterprise, from the first creative impulse to the last-night party.

'Three Friends', from Maltby and Shire's *Closer Than Ever*
(PHOTO: Ashley Straw)

1 · Where does it all begin?

At the heart of every theatrical enterprise there is a man or woman commonly known as the producer, who oversees the entire project from start to finish, and who has overall responsibility for putting the show together. This job is not for the faint-hearted, and requires a person with real passion for the project, good communication skills, and large amounts of energy and enthusiasm. In normal circumstances it is the producer who takes care of all the financial and organisational aspects of the production, and is therefore the business head of the project. The main responsibilities of the job are as follows.

- Drawing up a budget and organising all the production finances.
- Obtaining the performing rights and paying the appropriate fees to the licensing company.
- Selecting the creative team; director, musical director, choreographer, set designer, lighting designer, costume designer, and sound designer (if required).
- Arranging the appropriate back-up for the creative team, i.e. the stage management and technical personnel.
- Paying wages, if appropriate.
- Overseeing all aspects of publicity and advertising.
- Securing a suitable venue.
- Organising auditions and ensuring that rehearsal rooms are booked.
- Scheduling an overall timetable for the production.
- Inviting theatre critics from newspapers, magazines, television, and radio to the opening night.

It is often, though not always, the producer who dreams up the project to start with. Sometimes, however, a director will already be on board, and will help the producer to sift through the available material. There are, of course, hundreds and hundreds of musicals just waiting to be rediscovered, reinvented, and re-staged. There is also a rich pool of subjects to explore; from the sublime to the ridiculous, from the bizarre to the brain-numbingly banal. There are musicals about dogs, man-eating plants, and serial-killers; there are epic accounts of revolution and revolt, nuclear wars and presidential assassinations. There's even a musical about a certain little whore-house in Texas! The list goes on and on.

3

How to find the right show

At the start of the project, some producers will have a very strong idea about which show they wish to present. Others will need to do some searching. This can be achieved in a variety of ways. Some producers start at their public libraries and begin by sifting through musical scores, cast recordings, and videos of filmed musicals. Perhaps the most effective course of action, however, is to go straight to the publisher or licensing company and ask them to send out their show catalogue. Four companies which provide this service in England are Samuel French Ltd, MusicScope, Warner/Chappell Music Ltd, and Josef Weinberger Ltd (see appendix). Upon request, any of these organisations will send out information concerning their published musicals. This service is usually free, although several companies now charge a nominal fee. These catalogues contain useful information such as a brief description of the show, a breakdown of well-known songs from the score, and an indication of both cast requirements and orchestral numbers (see the example for *Guys and Dolls* below). Further information can be obtained by requesting 'perusal material', which usually includes both a vocal score and a libretto, and Music Theatre International, an American company (see appendix) also provides a unique service in the form of filmed conversations with the writers of selected musicals, such as Stephen Sondheim and Richard Maltby, Jr. This is currently available for a limited number of musicals, but will, I suspect, become a standard part of the research process in the future.

It is also worth noting that for an up-to-date list of shows available for amateur performance, application should be made to the National Operatic and Dramatic Association (NODA – see appendix). The list indicates which publisher

Music and lyrics by **Frank Loesser**, book by **Jo Swerling and Abe Burrows**, based on a story and characters by **Damon Runyon**

The improbable mixture of Miss Sarah Brown, a Salvation Army girl and Nathan Detroit, the operator of a floating crap game, gives us the main characters in this award-winning musical set in Times Square, Broadway. Unforgettable numbers include "Luck Be A Lady", "If I Were A Bell", "A Bushel And A Peck" and "Sit Down You're Rockin' The Boat".

Cast: 15 men, 4 women, chorus
Instrumentation: Reed I (piccolo [opt.]/flute [opt.]/clarinet/alto sax), Reed II (flute [opt.]/clarinet/alto sax/percussion [scratcher]), Reed III (oboe [opt.]/cor anglais [opt.]/clarinet/tenor sax), Reed IV (clarinet/ tenor sax), Reed V (bass clarinet/baritone sax/percussion [claves]), horn, 3 trumpets, trombone, percussion, piano, 4 violins, 2 cellos, double bass

An excerpt for *Guys and Dolls* from the Weinberger's catalogue
(courtesy of Josef Weinberger)

has the rights for which show, and gives contact numbers and addresses. Unfortunately there is no such service provided for those shows available for professional performance, and it is therefore best to contact the publishers or licensing company direct and ask for a copy of their show catalogue. (For further reference there is a list of musicals available for public performance on page 128.)

Once the producer (or director) has done some research into the different shows available for performance, he or she will start to eliminate some of these musicals due to lack of suitability. Although it may be tempting to limit the choice by weeding out any shows which appear to require large sets, expensive costumes, and complex lighting, I should stress that with a large amount of imagination, many problems of staging, lighting and costuming can be overcome very successfully. It really is true to say that you can achieve extraordinary results with 'a plank and a passion'; i.e., a space to perform in, and the determination and energy to put the whole show together. For this reason I am not of the opinion that the larger, more complicated musicals should be avoided at all costs, if there is little or no budget to play with. Some might say that to attempt a production of *South Pacific* or *My Fair Lady* with limited resources is to court disaster. On the contrary, I have seen, and been involved with several productions which have been hugely successful, despite having only a shoe-string budget. As has been seen time and time again in the West End and on Broadway, an abundance of money is no guarantee of success or quality. Likewise, the absence of money does not have to result in an impoverished production. Where a skilfully crafted show exists, it is, I believe, quite possible to present it with minimal costs in a highly effective and original manner.

I have recently worked on several student productions where the lack of budget forced us to be creative in a variety of different ways, resulting in some very interesting discoveries. An innovative production of the seventies musical *Two Gentlemen of Verona* (by Guare, Shapiro and MacDermot) was achieved with minimal lighting and set, and costumes which were begged, borrowed, and tie-dyed. Necessity forced us to be inventive, resulting in a style of production in which performers transformed themselves from Italian courtiers to trees, buses and thrones, in the blink of an eye. The sheer theatricality of this was tremendously exciting to watch and was the happy result of a non-existent budget. I strongly believe, therefore, that when choosing the right musical to present there are factors to take into consideration that are far more important than merely the apparent size and scale of a show.

Can the show be cast from the available pool of performers?

The first and most important question to ask is whether the actors who are likely to audition for the production have the necessary skills, both combined and individual, for this particular show. Are they primarily singers, dancers, or actors, or a combination of these disciplines? If you already have a show in mind, you should be reasonably sure before auditions begin that you will be able to fill the roles with sufficiently talented performers. It is no good trying to produce a production of *Fiddler on the Roof*, for example, if there are no suitable actors to play the taxing part of Tevye. Likewise, a production of *A Chorus Line* without an actress who can dance up a storm in the central role of Cassie is never going to work successfully since the character's dance ability is essential to the plot. I have already suggested that in many cases the staging difficulties in a production can often be overcome with great ingenuity and a dash of optimism. This is not, unfortunately, the case with actors, and there is absolutely no point in being unrealistic about the necessary talent required for certain productions. 'I'm sure that her range will expand in rehearsals', and 'We can easily teach him to tap in three weeks', are expectations which will probably land everybody in the soup.

It is also worth considering whether the chosen piece is suitable for the age group of the intended auditionees. If, for example, it is a school production, and the majority of the performers are teenagers, then clearly it is not a great idea to select shows such as Stephen Sondheim's *Follies*, or Cy Coleman's *On the Twentieth Century*, since these are musicals which feature older characters in the leading roles; parts which are probably going to be too taxing for the young actors to perform with credibility. On the other hand, *Grease* or *West Side Story* are perfect vehicles for young performers since in both cases they focus upon the joys and agonies of adolescence. Given the difficulties of staging a musical in the first place, it really does make sense to capitalise upon any natural advantages that you already have, such as the youth or maturity of the available performers.

It is also important, when deciding upon a particular show, to consider cast size. If you are intending to employ professional performers, how many actors can you afford? Can the actors double up on parts, thereby reducing numbers and consequent costs? Or, on the contrary, if the production is being presented at a school or college, are you aiming to include a whole class or a whole year in the show? Can the piece be expanded to incorporate extra characters on stage? A school production of *Oliver!*, for example, could work very well with an expanded ensemble, since there is no limit to the number of urchins that you could include.

The answers to these questions will only really be discovered by researching the piece thoroughly and working out the suitability of the show to your own specific requirements. Obviously if a musical relies for its effect upon having a large chorus, such as George Gershwin's *Crazy For You*, or Jerry Herman's *La Cage Aux Folles*, it would be unwise to attempt a scaled-down version for a handful of actors. However, if the piece is character-based, involving a large variety of different roles, it may be possible to cast it with half the number of actors, so that each performer plays two or more parts.

Is the musical suitable for the theatre or theatrical space available?

If the venue has already been fixed, this will also have a bearing on which show to choose. If it is a very flexible space, with moveable seating and large backstage areas, you may well find that it will be suitable for most productions. However, if it is a small theatre-in-the-round, with no orchestra pit and little extra stage space, then the band will have to be very small indeed, and this will inevitably affect your choice of show. A big, belty Broadway show like *Gypsy* or *Sweet Charity* will suffer enormously in these circumstances, since the power of these pieces is partly the result of the fabulous razzmatazz of the orchestrations. This is not to say that it is impossible to stage such shows in small venues, but there are probably other choices which would be more suitable, and ultimately more effective. On a similar note, it is clearly not sensible to choose a heavy dance show like *West Side Story* or *Anything Goes* if the theatrical space is cramped, or where there is no height to the stage, since dance leaps and lifts will be very difficult to achieve in these circumstances.

It is clearly a question of commonsense when it comes to matching the right show with the available venue, and as long as the producer is very clear as to the demands of a particular musical, then it should be a fairly straightforward process. Some matches are particularly delightful. A recent production of Sondheim's *The Frogs* was performed in a converted swimming-pool, a setting which provided the perfect ambience for this particular piece. On similar lines, a school gym might be the perfect environment for a production of *Grease*, where the majority of the actors play teenagers, or an old derelict warehouse might be a fabulous setting for *Sweeney Todd*.

A small student theatre provides a claustrophobic setting for a production of *Jack the Ripper* (PHOTO: Nick Davey)

Is the musical suitable for the intended audience?

This is obviously a question which will particularly preoccupy the producer, and one which must be given some attention. If the audience is likely to be full of children and teenagers, then it may be wise to opt for the more upbeat, contemporary shows such as *The Wiz*, or *Fame – The Musical*, rather than the more sophisticated subject matter of Sondheim's *Company*, for example. Likewise, older audiences may prefer the comfortable familiarity of *Oklahoma!* or *The King and I*. This is not to say, however, that an older audience may not love a production of *The Wiz*, or that a younger crowd may not find *Oklahoma!* an enthralling experience. It is for the producer to decide, and having taken into consideration the age group and social background of the potential audience, he or she must decide whether to play safe, or to throw caution to the winds. Unfortunately, financial considerations will often ensure that the former course of action is taken.

Performing rights

Once a firm decision has been made about which musical to produce, the next step is to apply for the performing rights. This application is usually made to the publisher, or to the company which holds the performing rights; the licensing company. Although there are minor differences between applying for amateur and professional rights, the process is essentially the same and should be approached in a similar way. Upon application, the producer will be expected to provide a certain amount of information, such as performance dates, number of performances, venue, seating capacity, and ticket prices. There are various reasons why an application may be turned down, but it is usually because another production of the same show is due to take place at the same time. The rights for a show will also often be withheld if a national tour or West End production is in the pipe-line, or currently in performance.

If the application is accepted, the publisher and the producer will sign an agreement licensing the production to go ahead, and confirming all practical details of the show, including royalty payments and hire charges for scores and librettos, etc. The producer will also accept certain conditions stipulated by the contract, which will usually include an agreement that no changes can be made to the script or score without prior consent from the writer's estate.

In my experience, publishers are often surprisingly flexible when it comes to the orchestration of the musical. Most producers, particularly where amateur and fringe shows are concerned, are simply unable to afford the full complement of musicians stipulated for any given show. It is often the case, however, that alternative arrangements already exist for smaller numbers of instrumentalists or 'musical combos' as they are often called, and these can be obtained directly from the publishers. There is usually also an arrangement for two pianos, which may not provide the ideal accompaniment, but will be a much more economical option for many producers.

So, once the licence has been signed, and decisions have been made about the

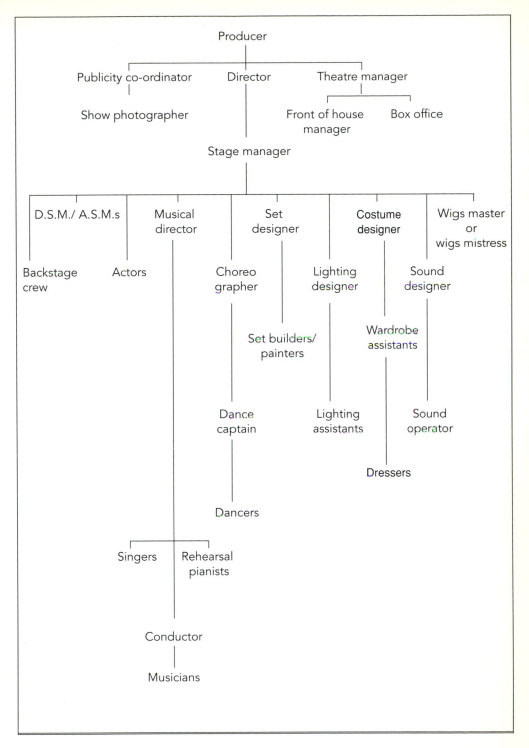

type of orchestration required, the producer should inform the publishers of the rehearsal dates so that rehearsal material such as librettos and musical scores can be sent out to arrive by the appropriate date. It is usual for the band parts to arrive at a later stage, but if for any reason the musical director requires them earlier in rehearsals, the publisher should be notified as soon as possible. The licence also dictates certain stipulations regarding the printed information on posters and programmes, and often the publishers will expect to see proofs so that the credits can be checked before going to print. Once the production goes into performance, the producer will be expected to send box-office receipts to the publisher so that royalty payments can be assessed. The agreement will also specify that scripts and scores are returned by a certain date, and that the publisher is reimbursed for any material which is damaged or lost.

This is only a brief account of the contract between the producer and the publishing house/licensing company, and there are many finer details which I have not included in this summary, and which will only become clear to the producer once he or she enters into a dialogue with the publisher. In my experience most publishers are more than happy to explain the procedure to the uninitiated, and will take time to discuss the details of the contract in order to clarify the whole process.

So, once the producer has secured the rights for the show (or at least checked with the publisher to ensure that the proposed musical is available) he or she will start to gather a production team together. As has already been suggested, the producer is ultimately in charge of the whole production and has overall responsibility for every other member of the team. The accountability chart on the previous page gives some indication of the responsibilities of each member of the production team and also shows the links between each department.

2 · The creative team

It is usually the producer who will decide on a suitable director for the project. Often he or she will already be acquainted with the director, and will be fairly familiar with his or her working methods. Sometimes, however, the director is known by reputation only, and may have been recommended for the job by a third party. In such a case it is important for the producer to meet and talk with the prospective director before any firm decisions are made. After all, they will be in constant contact throughout the production, and it is vital, therefore, that they are able to communicate well, and that their basic aims are the same.

For a recent production of Maltby and Shire's *Closer Than Ever*, I was approached by the producer through a mutual contact, and we met to discuss the project in some detail before I was finally asked to work on the show. We then set about gathering together the creative team and the production personnel that we would require. In my experience this is usually the way that the selection procedure works. Certainly from my point of view, as a director, I am much happier if I can have some input as far as the choice of musical director, choreographer, and design team is concerned. Of course, in many school or college productions, there is often a limited choice of personnel, and there may be only one person with the necessary skills to design sets, or conduct the orchestra, or choreograph the dance numbers.

Once the creative team has been assembled, someone must have overall artistic control of the production, and this should be the director. There is no point in pretending that the theatre is some sort of wonderful creative democracy, because ultimately someone has to make the decisions, and although a good director will always listen carefully to every member of the team, he or she will sometimes have to use some directorial authority to get things done. I am not advocating an artistic dictatorship, but merely suggesting that the director should be someone who can bring together all the creative elements of the production and therefore ensure that everyone is working towards the same artistic goals.

Once the creative team has been selected, it is most important that everybody meets to discuss the show, and the possible ways of approaching the production. These meetings are called 'production meetings', and should continue at regular intervals during the pre-production period and throughout rehearsals. Later meetings will include members of the other departments such as the stage management, and the publicity department. These early creative discussions will usually take place between the following people; the director, the musical director, the choreographer, the set designer, the lighting designer, and the costume designer. If there is a sound designer involved in the project, he or she will probably attend later production meetings. It is usual for the producer to be present in these early discussions, but not always essential.

The director

Just as the producer is really the business head of the production, the director should be considered as the artistic head. Although much of the job will involve working with the actors in the rehearsal room, there is a large amount of planning needed to ensure that everything goes as smoothly as possible. Most importantly, the director must always be aware of everything that is going on in the other departments. For this reason, he or she must communicate well with the other members of the creative team, and must make sure that they are kept up-to-date with the latest developments in the rehearsal room. The stage manager will also help to achieve this. Other main responsibilities include:

- Studying the piece, and making overall decisions about style and interpretation based on discussions with other members of the artistic team.
- Casting the show, usually with the assistance of the producer, the musical director and the choreographer.
- Organising an overall schedule for the rehearsal period.
- Rehearsing the actors, giving background information on the piece, and helping to develop characterisations, etc.
- Overseeing all artistic aspects of the show throughout the rehearsal period, communicating with the various different departments involved in the production, and ensuring artistic unity throughout the project.
- Providing material for the programme, if required, and helping to publicise the show by giving interviews to the press, radio, or television.
- Maintaining the show once it has opened; attending performances, giving notes to the cast, and re-rehearsing problem areas, if necessary.
- Rehearsing understudies, if required, or delegating this task to an assistant director or in some cases to the stage manager.

The musical director

The musical director (more commonly known as the MD) is, of course, responsible for all aspects of music in the show. Not only will the MD work with the actors in the rehearsal room, but he or she will be fully in charge of the orchestra, or band, and will rehearse these musicians separately until the 'sitzprobe' (i.e., the sing-through involving both actors and musicians; see Chapter 10). For this reason, there will often be an assistant musical director who can be present in the rehearsal room, while the main MD is busy working with the band. In detail, the MD is responsible for:

- Organising (with the help of the producer) a pianist for auditions and rehearsals.
- Attending auditions and advising the director on the casting of the singers.
- Teaching the cast their vocal parts and helping to solve any musical problems which the singers may have.
- If required, making a rehearsal tape for the choreographer of all the dance music in the show.
- Selecting the band or orchestra (in larger productions this may be done by a 'fixer'), and rehearsing the musicians.
- Conducting the band or orchestra in performance.
- Organising vocal warm-ups for the cast during the run, and ensuring that musical standards are maintained. This may involve calling the cast for extra vocal rehearsals.

The choreographer

The choreographer will be in charge of all the dance sections of the show. He or she may also be involved in other aspects of staging or blocking. This will depend upon the personalities of the people involved, and the degree of help required by the director. The main choreographic responsibilities are as follows.

- Researching and developing dance ideas after initial discussions with the director.
- Attending auditions, devising a suitable dance routine for these auditions, and advising the director about the casting of dancers.
- Supervising dance warm-ups in rehearsal, and helping to maintain the physical fitness of the cast.
- Choreographing all of the danced sections of the show, and helping with staging and blocking if required.
- Selecting a dance captain (a member of the company who will help drill the dance numbers and perhaps take physical warm-ups in the absence of the choreographer).
- Maintaining the standard of dance when the show is in performance by attending the show, taking notes, and calling extra rehearsals, if required.

The design team

The design team usually consists of the set designer, the costume designer, and the lighting designer. On larger musicals, especially those being produced in a sizeable theatre, there will often also be a sound designer. It is not unusual for the set design and the costume design to be done by the same person, and there are many situations where jobs can be doubled up very successfully. For example, the director will also sometimes design the lighting, or choreograph the dance numbers. It is very important that there is good communication between each member of the design team, and that any changes that are made during rehearsals are quickly relayed to each department. For example, if a brightly coloured rug is suddenly required by the director for a certain scene, the costume designer will want to make sure that anyone sitting on the rug will not be wearing something that will clash horribly with the colour. Usually, in such a situation, the designer will discuss the options with the costume designer, and they will come up with a solution. Basically, no man is an island when it comes to putting on a show, and as long as there is good communication between departments, all should go fairly smoothly.

The set designer

The set designer is responsible for the overall look of the show, and will need to work closely with both the costume designer and the lighting designer. He or she is usually also responsible for both the set-dressing and the props. Other areas of the job include:

- Liaising with the director and making clear decisions about the piece from an early stage; i.e., the period of the show, whether it is to be naturalistic or stylised, and how many scene changes will be required.

- Where necessary, doing detailed research on the period in which the piece is to be set, and collecting useful information regarding architecture, furniture, etc., which will help in creating a design concept.

- Drawing a story-board – a series of pictures which represent each different stage setting – so that the director can clearly see how each scene will be realised.

- Making a model box to scale, and presenting it to the cast on the first day of rehearsals.

- Overseeing the building of the set.

- Supervising the buying of props (both set-dressing and personal props) and liaising with the stage manager in case any aspects of the design need altering during rehearsals.

- If required, having an input when it comes to deciding upon a design for the poster and the programme.

The lighting designer

No lighting designer can begin to light a show without detailed discussion with the set designer, the costume designer and the director about style, interpretation and colour. The effectiveness of the lighting will depend enormously on the colours and textures used by the set and costume designers, and therefore good communication between these departments is vital. The lighting designer will also need to be supplied with a detailed plan of the set as early as possible so that he or she can begin to decide where to hang specific lights in order to achieve the desired lighting effects. The chief duties of the lighting designer are:

- After suitable discussion with the director and the other members of the design team, determining the style of lighting required for the production and discussing any possible special effects which may be needed.

- Devising a preliminary lighting plot for the show.

- Liaising with the stage management and determining how to achieve certain effects with smoke machines, dry ice machines, pyrotechnical flashes, etc.

- Compiling a detailed list of lighting requirements and providing a plan showing the exact placement of the lights in the theatre.

- Ordering the necessary equipment from the suppliers, supervising the rigging of the lights in the theatre, and when in position, focusing these lights.

- Using the devised lighting plot as a guide, plotting in sequence all the lighting states for the show. (These will need to be programmed into a computer, and cued by the stage management during the performance.)

- Maintaining the quality of the lighting by attending performances, taking notes, and ensuring that the lights are refocused and replaced when necessary.

The costume designer

Although the main task facing the costume designer is to provide suitable costumes for all of the characters in the production, his or her job tends to spill over into other areas, especially on smaller productions where budgets are tight and resources are limited. Often the costume designer will also help to coordinate wigs and hair-pieces, if required, and will usually assist with jewellery and accessories such as hats, gloves and bags. Unless a make-up artist is specifically required for special effects (and in my experience this is fairly unusual) the costume designer will also often help with make-up, giving the actors a clear idea of the type of 'look' required for each character. The main responsibilities of the costume designer are as follows.

- After discussion with the director and the other members of the design team, researching in detail the period of the show, and starting to collect together design ideas, e.g., fabrics, colours, and patterns.

- Drawing up a list of measurements for each member of the cast, preferably before rehearsals begin.

- Providing a costume plot for each character in the show. Where costumes are being made, this will often be accompanied by costume sketches, and perhaps samples of the appropriate fabric.

- Where necessary, organising and supervising the making of costumes.

- Arranging for the hiring of costumes, if required.

- Arranging fittings, once the costumes have been made or hired, and supervising any alterations that may be required.

- Where necessary, providing temporary costumes for rehearsals: these may include 'practice' skirts, and assorted hats, shawls, gloves, etc.

- Organising a costume parade once the costumes are available, so that the director can see the overall effect.

- Appointing a wardrobe master or mistress who will look after the costumes during the run of the show, supervise the maintenance of the costumes, (including cleaning and ironing) and return all hired costumes after the final performance. In smaller-scale productions, the costume designer will usually take on these tasks too.

The sound designer

The idea of a sound designer may appear to be rather an odd concept, but as musical productions become more sophisticated, and bands become larger or more synthesised, there is often the need for some sort of amplification. In these cases it is not simply the voices that need to be miked, it may also be the individual members of the band as well. This in turn often leads to the need for loud-speakers, so that the performers can actually hear themselves above the amplified band. If this sounds complicated, well it is! Hence the need for a sound designer. In many circumstances, however, amplification is simply an added complication and an unnecessary expense, and I have seen many successful productions which have relied solely upon the power of the actors' voices and the acoustics of the venue. In fact, bad amplification is invariably worse than no amplification at all, and it is really only worth considering using radio mikes and all the paraphernalia that accompanies them if the budget can stretch to equipment of a high standard. However, where amplification *is* required, it is extremely important to have someone skilled in charge of the whole procedure. The role of a sound designer is:

- To discuss the style of the show and its musical content with the director and the musical director, and to decide upon a suitable approach to sound design.

- To assess the natural acoustics of the theatre or performance space and to decide how best to amplify the sound, if amplification is required.

- To oversee the hiring of all sound equipment, and to supervise its installation in the theatre.

- To liaise with the director and the stage manager, and to provide all the appropriate sound effects for the production.

- To supervise the 'sound check' in the theatre (the period allocated for adjusting sound levels, mixing the sound, etc.).

- Where necessary (usually when a complicated sound design is required) to appoint sound operators to mix the sound during the show, and to supervise all aspects of sound during the run.

- To maintain the quality of the sound during the run by attending performances, making notes, and fixing problems as and when they arise.

3 · Stage management and technical support

Once the producer has gathered together a suitable creative team for the project, it is time to start thinking about appointing the stage management. This term is, I think, a rather inadequate description of a job which is multi-faceted and which brings with it a whole range of responsibilities. Of all the jobs in the theatre, this is perhaps the hardest to define, since the responsibilities of the stage management team will usually vary to some degree from job to job. This team of people will provide a vital support mechanism for the creative team and for the actors, and will, in a very practical sense, organise the day-to-day running of rehearsals, and ultimately of performances too. The importance of stage management cannot be over-emphasised, since it provides the practical foundation upon which the production is built, and is absolutely vital to the smooth running of the whole process. Great care should be taken when selecting this team, and special attention should be paid to the appointment of the overall head of this department – the stage manager.

The size of the stage management team will of course depend upon the complexity of the show. It is usual to have at least two members of this team, a stage manager (SM) and a deputy stage manager (DSM), and any number of assistant stage managers (ASMs) can be added to this core.

In my experience the best stage managers are invariably good communicators; they are observant, quick-thinking, and efficient, and, perhaps most important, they are always reliable in a crisis. A good sense of humour is a valuable asset too, since the job has more than its fair share of stresses and strains. For work on a musical it is certainly an advantage if the stage manager has some musical knowledge, and whoever cues the show during performance (this is usually the DSM) will have to be able to find his or her way around a musical score.

Ideally the stage manager should work in close contact with the director throughout the whole process, and together they should try to ensure that rehearsal time is used as productively as possible. At best a good stage manager is an unflappable problem-solver who deals with all sorts of difficulties calmly and efficiently as and when they arise. By shouldering most of the practical responsibilities, the stage manager allows the director to concentrate on making the artistic decisions, and ensures that the rehearsals are as stress-free as possible. In short, the stage manager should be in charge of the running of the rehearsal room, and should ultimately be responsible for the smooth running of the show in performance. He or she will be helped in these matters by the other members of the stage management team, but will ultimately have to take overall responsibility for the whole department.

Stage management duties

The following list of job responsibilities indicates just how diverse the job of stage management can be. There is also a string of smaller tasks, too numerous to mention, which will also be part of the duties of the stage management team. Since the requirements for every production differ to some degree, nobody can foresee all the possible problems that may arise during rehearsals and performance. But with a reliable stage management team, comprised of people with lots of initiative and a flexible approach to their work, most of these difficulties can easily be overcome. The main responsibilities are as follows:

At the planning stage
- Helping to organise auditions, ensuring that a piano is available (and in tune), and making sure that the necessary scores and scripts are to hand.
- Helping the director to devise a provisional rehearsal schedule.
- Ensuring that rehearsal rooms are well equipped, adequately proportioned, and suitable for the purposes of the specific show. For example, if the show requires dance sequences, is there a mirrored wall in the rehearsal space?
- After consultation with the designer, ensuring that the rehearsal room is marked out with tape to show the exact dimensions of the stage space.

In the rehearsal room
- Compiling a contact sheet and distributing it to all members of the cast and production team.
- Providing rehearsal props for the actors (until the actual show props have been acquired). Also providing suitable furniture such as chairs, tables, desks, etc.
- Compiling comprehensive lists of props and sound effects.
- Prompting during rehearsals, if required by the actors.
- Taking accurate timings for each act during rehearsals.
- Keeping a 'marked up' copy of the script and music (called the prompt book), and noting in it the moves of the actors, and the cue points for sound effects, scene changes, special effects etc.
- Ensuring that the rehearsal room remains a productive place of work (i.e., that it is clean, well heated or well ventilated, and available for use whenever the actors are called).

- Checking that the performers know the times of their calls, arrive punctually to rehearsals and have regular breaks. Also ensuring that the actors get to and from photo calls, publicity interviews, etc. and making sure that they attend costume fittings during rehearsals.

During production week
- Coordinating and running the technical and dress rehearsals in the theatre, and ensuring that the production schedule is followed as closely as possible.
- Organising the cast once the production moves from the rehearsal room to the theatre, and taking charge of dressing-room allocation. Also setting up a signing-in sheet for the actors (to check attendance), and issuing calls to the stage (the half-hour call, the five minute call, etc.).

During the run
- Notifying the front-of-house manager when the auditorium may be opened to the public, and announcing cast changes to the audience, if necessary. Also addressing the audience if, for any reason, the show is interrupted, delayed, or cancelled.
- Cueing the show in performance from the 'prompt desk', and signalling when scene changes, lighting changes and sound cues should take place.
- Organising and taking responsibility for the backstage areas: helping with scene changes; handing props to the actors; helping with speedy costume changes (in the absence of dressers).
- Maintaining the show during its run. This includes checking that damaged props are mended; ensuring that supplies of perishable props (food, drink, etc.) are constantly replaced; generally maintaining the set, and reporting to any of the separate departments (design, lighting, etc.) when there are problems in their specific areas.
- Calling the performers to the stage for their entrances, if necessary (theatres very often have a show relay playing in the dressing-rooms during the performance, so individual calls are unnecessary).
- Checking that the show starts on time, keeping an accurate account of the playing time of each act, and monitoring the length of each interval.
- Keeping a written account of all problems, technical and artistic, which occur during the run, and also providing an 'accident book' to record any physical injuries which may be sustained during the show.

After the run
- Helping to strike the set, ensuring that all scripts and scores are returned to the publisher, and checking that the theatre is left in a reasonable state.

It is perhaps worth noting that on larger-scale productions the stage management team often expands to include a production manager and a company stage manager. Although I do not intend to go into these jobs in great detail, I will briefly outline their duties:

- The production manager takes responsibility for the technical planning of the production and ensures that the technical departments keep within budget and meet the agreed deadlines for completion of their work.

- The company stage manager is usually only required in commercial theatres, or in larger repertory theatres. He or she will take overall responsibility for the running of the show; will oversee the payment of wages and the monitoring of box office receipts; and will discipline the theatre staff and the performers if the need should arise.

The stage crew

In addition to the stage management, most productions will require the services of a stage crew. This is a team of people who initially will help to construct the set in the theatre, help with the rigging of lights, and generally act as assistants to the stage manager. During performance they will usually assist with scene changes: manning the fly towers if scenery is to be flown in and out; operating follow spots; moving stage furniture and other equipment; and on some productions operating stage revolves, trap doors, etc.

4 · Budgets, schedules and publicity

There is no getting round it: compared with a straight play, the musical is costly and complicated to produce, mainly because it involves a unique combination of different disciplines; music, drama, and often dance too. It is expensive to produce for various reasons. Firstly, it often requires larger numbers of performers than the straight play and therefore more expenditure on costume, make-up, etc. In addition, it always requires some sort of musical accompaniment, whether this comes in the form of an orchestra, a band, or simply a piano. In my experience, even when the show is produced in a semi-professional capacity, musicians will usually require some sort of payment, and in the case of a band or orchestra, this can amount to a large percentage of the budget. Even when the musical accompaniment is limited to a single piano, there are often extra costs to consider, such as payment for transporting the piano, or for maintenance and tuning during rehearsals and performance (in some cases this can be as often as once a week). Also, if larger numbers of musicians are required, the actors on stage will often need to be amplified, whether by means of radio mikes, or other strategically-placed microphones. This can be a very costly procedure, and for this reason, decisions about sound enhancement should be made at an early stage in the whole process.

So, if money and resources are really tight, it is well worth thinking twice before making the commitment to produce a musical. As I mentioned in Chapter 1, money is no guarantee of success, and a tight budget can often force the production team to come up with some very creative ideas. However, there are some areas in which under-funding may seriously affect the project as a whole. If the music budget is very tight, the result may well be a second-rate band, and on a show that relies heavily on music, this can seriously impoverish the whole production. Likewise, if the lighting budget is minimal, the finished product may look cheap and under-produced. These are just two areas where under-funding may have a very detrimental effect on the overall production.

Drawing up a budget

Once the producer has decided which show to produce, where to produce it, and for how long, he or she must draw up a realistic budget for the entire production. The emphasis here is upon the word *realistic*, since it is all too easy to launch into a production with great enthusiasm and energy, but to forget about the practical details concerning the financing of the project. The producer, being the business head of the team, should try to ensure that the budget is drawn up as accurately as possible, and should avoid approaching the enterprise in an over-optimistic, rose-tinted fashion. The creative team can afford to go off on wild flights of fancy, but the producer cannot. In fact, the producer must always have one eye firmly fixed on the practical details of the production, while also allowing members of the artistic team to exercise their imaginations as creatively as possible.

When drawing up a budget, the producer will need to assess both the possible income from the project, and the likely expenditure. Clearly if the outgoings exceed the potential income, there will need to be some financial support from another source. This may come in the shape of a subsidy from a local council, a donation from a benefactor, or a sum of money invested in the production by an 'angel'. This term applies to an investor who will expect to see some return for the investment if the production goes into profit and is, of course, only applicable to a professional show.

In the budget sheet shown on page 24 I have not attempted to give any specific idea of the actual sums of money to be allocated to each department, since this will of course differ hugely depending upon the type of show, the overall budget available, and the producer's own assessment of where the financial priorities lie. Although the budget sheet appears to be fairly straightforward, there are several aspects which need to be investigated further.

Production costs and running costs

It is important to remember, especially where longer runs are concerned, that expenditure does not suddenly cease once the performance is up and running. There are many areas of the show which will need to be maintained. Costumes, for example, will require cleaning and repairing; lights will sometimes need to be replaced; the set may need repainting and will almost certainly require some maintenance, and props will need to be repaired or replaced (certain of these, such as food, drink and fresh flowers, will need to be replaced on a daily basis).

Respecting the budget

Ideally the budget will have been drawn up by the producer once he or she has assessed the financial requirements of the piece and has discussed the project with the head of each department. It is most important that the figures that are finally set must be agreed by each department to be practical for the amount of material and work required. There is no point in a producer presenting an unrealistic budget and expecting the costume department to create fifty costumes, or the publicity department to produce five hundred posters, for next to nothing. Once the figure has been agreed, however, it is the responsibility of the head of each department to respect this budget and to ensure that over-spending does not occur.

Budget sheet

Income
Ticket sales
Programme and merchandising sales
Advertising in programme
Gifts from sponsors and investors
Grants from local authorities, etc.

Expenditure
Royalties (agreed with the licensing company)
Salaries for employees (if applicable)
Rental fees for scripts, scores, etc.
Hire of venue
Set (including materials, construction, and transportation)
Costumes, wigs, accessories, and costume maintenance
Props
Lighting
Sound (if applicable)
Make-up (in most cases supplied by the actors)
Renting audition rooms and rehearsal rooms
Hiring and tuning pianos for rehearsals and performances
Publicity (including posters, flyers, newspaper adverts)
Printing of tickets and programmes
Production photographer and photos
Administrative costs (telephone, postage, etc.)
Insurance (if not covered by the theatre)
First night party
Contingency

Reviewing the budget

It is not enough to set out a budget at the start of the production informing each department of its specific financial allocation, and then to expect the whole thing to run like clockwork. Budgets should be reviewed at regular intervals and, if necessary, altered to suit the changing needs of the production. Maybe the costume department decide not to use any wigs, but to dress the performers' hair instead. The money saved in this area may be reallocated to the lighting department, for example, to help pay for a much needed stroboscope or a flashing neon sign. As long as the producer keeps a watchful eye on the finances in each department and reallocates when necessary, he or she should be able to solve many problems without having to search for extra funding from elsewhere.

Contingency

Since there are always hidden costs involved in mounting a production of any type, it is sensible to set aside a reasonable amount for unforeseen expenses or 'contingency'. These hidden costs can be the result of artistic changes made during rehearsals, and they can be as minor as an extra hat or jacket for one of the cast, or as major as a chaise-longue, a revolving door, or a working motorcar. While it is to be hoped that the director will not make unnecessary demands once the budget has been allocated, it is inevitable that some expenses will arise which have not been anticipated. The contingency money is there to cover these unexpected costs and must be guarded carefully so that it is available if a department is forced to go over budget for some reason. It also comes in handy for more mundane eventualities, such as the cost of a cab to a radio interview for one of the cast, or the cost of bottled water for the cast during performance.

As a final word on budgets, it is perhaps worth mentioning that theatre people, as a general rule, are not terribly good with finances. Since the process of mounting a musical requires enormous energy and positive commitment, there is often an over-riding feeling of optimism – a sense that by hook or by crook the show will go on. Of course much can be achieved with a positive outlook, and it is extraordinary how much one can beg and borrow when money is tight. It is important, however, to try to temper enthusiasm with a realistic attitude towards finance, and the producer must be the one to keep a practical head at all times.

Scheduling

From the moment that the actors pick up their scripts on the first day of rehearsals, the countdown begins and the pressure is on. Everyone knows that deadlines in the theatre have to be met, and the biggest deadline of all is the first public performance. Cancellations do, of course, occur from time to time, but they are to be avoided at all costs, since they are financially disastrous for the producer, extremely disappointing for the theatre audience, and unnerving for the actors. A realistic schedule is, therefore, one way to ensure that the show will go on.

Although in some circumstances (a school or college production, for example) rehearsals can be flexible and unhurried, with most theatre work, the scheduling of rehearsals, technical work, dress rehearsals, and first performances is crucial to the success of the whole venture. It is with the latter situation in mind that I am investigating this subject.

For a professional production (whether this be rep, fringe, or West End) the producer will usually schedule the rehearsals according to the date of the opening night. To ensure that the production is covered by the press, the producer will usually contact the Society Of London Theatre (SOLT – see appendix) to check the press night diary, and to determine whether other theatre performances are opening on the same evening. Obviously if a large number of shows are opening on the same day, the chance of being reviewed becomes less likely. Once the producer has fixed the date of the opening night and informed SOLT of the decision, he or she can then work backwards, fitting in preview performances, technical and dress rehearsals, the theatre 'get-in' and 'fit-up', and the rehearsals.

There is no golden rule when it comes to allocating sufficient time for rehearsing a musical. In my experience four or five weeks is generally adequate for a standard two to three hour show. I have, however, been involved in projects which have rehearsed for much longer (three months in one case!), and still panic has set in at the approach of the first performance. At best a generous rehearsal period enables the director and the acting company to experiment with the material, and to really get to grips with the music, the script, and the choreography. At worst, it results in a lazy approach to the work, and a general lack of focus.

The director and artistic team will usually be in favour of a longer rehearsal period, since this enables them to have more time to work creatively on the project, while the producer, mainly for financial reasons, usually favours a tighter schedule. Ultimately some sort of compromise is always reached. It is very important, however, that all the departments agree on the feasibility of the schedule; there is no point in a producer imposing a two week rehearsal period on a show like *My Fair Lady*, which clearly requires longer to stage.

In every area of the performing arts there is bound to be some degree of creative guesswork involved in scheduling rehearsals, since there are so many variables to consider. No two actors will work at the same speed, no two singers will learn their vocal parts in quite the same way, and every director will have a different approach to staging a show. Once everyone on the production team has agreed to the proposed rehearsal plan, however, it is up to each of them to ensure that their specific responsibilities are taken care of, and that their department has fulfilled its role by the time the show goes into performance.

It is perhaps simplest to think of the production schedule as working in two stages. Stage 1 covers the period between the first day of rehearsals and the final run-through in the rehearsal room, and Stage 2 covers the period between the get-in (access to the theatre) and the opening night. The producer will ultimately make the decision as to how much time is needed on Stage 1 and Stage 2, but this decision should be reached in consultation with the other members of the production team. If, for example, the show requires radio mikes for the singers, there will need to be more stage time available to balance the sound. Likewise, if the scenery is complex and the show requires many scene changes, then the schedule will have to take this into consideration. Every production has different requirements, and scheduling decisions must be tailor-made to suit the specific show in hand.

In my experience, once the production moves from the rehearsal room to the theatre there never seems to be quite enough time to achieve perfect results in every department. Since economically it does not make sense to keep a theatre 'dark' for any length of time (this refers to the period when no show is actually in performance), the time allocated to Stage 2 often seems to be very limited, and it is vital that everything is well organised at this stage and that no time is wasted. The schedule for a production of *Oklahoma!* illustrated opposite indicates how careful planning can utilize the available stage time to the full.

OKLAHOMA! - PRODUCTION SCHEDULE

		Arts Theatre		**Rehearsal Room**
Monday 21st May	9.00	Technical Work		
	10.00	Company Rehearsal on Stage (with piano/no costumes)		
	13.00	Lunch		
	14.00	Actors into Costume	14.00	Orchestra Rehearsal with Conductor
	14.30	Company on Stage for Tech 1 (with piano)	18.00	Orchestra Call to finish
	18.00	Supper		
	19.00	Company on Stage for Tech 2 (with piano)		
	23.00	All work to finish		

		Arts Theatre		**Rehearsal Room**
Tuesday 22nd May	9.00	Technical Work		
	9.30	Actors into Costume		
	10.00	Company on Stage for Tech 3 (with piano)		
	13.00	Lunch		
	14.00	Company on Stage for Tech 4 (with piano)	14.00	Orchestra Rehearsal with Conductor
	18.00	Supper	18.00	Orchestra Call to finish
	19.00	Company on Stage for Sound Balance/Music Call		
	23.00	All work to finish		

		Arts Theatre		**Rehearsal Room**
Wednesday 23rd May	9.00	Technical Work		
	10.00	Extra tech session, if required		
	13.00	Lunch		
	14.00	Actors into Costume		
	14.30	Company on Stage for Dress Rehearsal 1		
	18.00	Supper		
	19.00	Notes with Director		
	20.00	Company on Stage for Dress Rehearsal 2		
	23.00	All work to finish		

Stage 1

Although I shall go into greater detail about the specific planning of the rehearsal schedule in Chapter 8, the main objectives during Stage 1 are as follows.

- To rehearse in detail every aspect of the show, ensuring that the script, the music, the choreography, and the staging are all learned and memorised.

- To work towards a series of final runs in the rehearsal room, where the musical can run as smoothly as possible, with every performer 'off the book' (i.e., having memorised the lines).

Stage 2

This is a time of frenetic activity when all the different strands of the production are pulled together for the first time. In most cases, musicals will require a longer preparation period in the theatre than straight plays because of the added complication of seating the orchestra, balancing the sound, restaging dance routines and so on. The main objectives of Stage 2 are:

- To construct the set in the theatre and to finish work on it by the time the actors appear on stage.

- To rig the lighting equipment in the theatre, to focus the lights, and to plot the lighting states for the show.

- To install the sound equipment (if required), and to balance the sound between the orchestra or band and the actors on stage.

- To rehearse the show technically, ensuring that the actors are comfortable with all aspects of staging, and to ensure that all props are tried, tested, and approved.

- To run the show in a dress rehearsal situation, with props, costumes, lighting, sound, and full orchestra or band.

Most professional productions will schedule some previews into Stage 2 of the production schedule. These are early performances which are open to the public, normally at a reduced rate, and are usually considered to be 'work in progress' since changes are often made from one show to the next. The production does not usually settle until the opening night.

Publicity

Just as the budget and the production schedule both need to be drawn up long before the actors set foot in the rehearsal room, so too is it important to plan the show's publicity at an early stage. After all, there is no point in creating a great production if nobody comes to see it. In a professional production there will

A publicity photo for a production of Maltby and Shire's *Starting Here, Starting Now* (PHOTO: Ashley Straw)

usually be someone employed to take care of publicity, but in the case of fringe work, or community or amateur projects, the responsibility for selling the show will probably land squarely on the shoulders of the producer.

The main areas of responsibility for anyone undertaking the publicity for a show are as follows.

- Supervising the production of posters and flyers, ensuring that they have all the relevant information on them, and organising printing.

- Overseeing the distribution of posters and flyers to shops, restaurants, schools, libraries, community centres, other theatres, etc.

- Taking out advertisements in local newspapers and magazines, and contacting local television and radio stations to inform them about the production.

- Sending press releases to newspapers and magazines, including all relevant information about the production.

- Where possible, contacting local shops to organise window displays featuring such items as posters and photos from the production.

- Supervising the production and printing of theatre programmes. In some cases the publicity supervisor will also sell advertising space in the programme.

There are, of course, other ways of publicising a production, such as taking the actors out onto the streets, performing excerpts from the show, and handing out flyers to interested members of the public. Often a producer will also publicise the show by contacting local schools and drama schools directly (especially if the musical has some specific relevance to the course work) and offering discounts to groups of students.

It is sometimes possible to get pre-show publicity from local newspapers by focusing on a specific aspect of the production, and by providing unusual photographs, or a quirky story which is in some way connected with the show. For example, a production of *Iolanthe* which I directed several years ago required a life-size male statue for one of the scenes. A female display mannequin was donated by a local shop, so the props department had to set about giving the dummy a sex change! For some reason, the local press thought that this was a great story, and provided us with some very useful publicity, well before the production actually opened.

Posters

For most productions (excluding the very high budget shows which can afford extensive newspaper, radio and even television advertisements), the single most important aspect of publicity is the poster. Ideally this should tie in stylistically with the production itself and should give some idea to the public about the type of show that it is advertising. It is well worth taking time and effort over the poster, since it really can create a buzz about the show if it is well designed and well distributed. There are several vital pieces of information which must be included on the poster and flyers:

- The name of the society or production company.

- The title of the show.

- The names of the writers, lyricists and composers.

- The venue.

- The dates and times of the performances.

- The price of tickets, and where to obtain them (concessions should also be indicated).

- Any information provided by the licensing company expressly for publicity purposes. According to the contract certain details must be included on the

poster (these often include information about the original director/choreographer).

In some cases the producer will want to include the names of the individual members of the creative team, and the names of some or all of the performers on the poster. Indeed in some professional shows the producer may be contractually obliged to do this if such an agreement has been reached with the actors' agents. Also if the show is an amateur one, the contract with the licensing company will specify that this fact is clearly indicated on all advertisements.

Usually the flyer, or handbill, is a smaller version of the poster. It will probably not include quite so much information on the front, but will normally have a fairly detailed description of the show on the back, and will include details about the cast and the creative team.

Programmes

Assuming that the publicity has been effective, and that an audience has been enticed into the theatre, it is most important that there is a reasonably priced, informative programme for the public to purchase before seeing the show. This will often use for its cover a similar, or identical, design to the poster.

The contents of theatre programmes vary enormously, and there are no particular set rules here (except the inclusion of various bits of information specified by the licensing company in the contract). However, most programmes will include a cast list, specifying which characters are played by which actors, and a list of other personnel involved in the production. Also it is usual to include biographies of the cast, the production team, and the writers. There may also be a synopsis of the story (although this is becoming less common, and is frankly unnecessary for most musicals). Sometimes the songs will be listed in order, and often the programme will specify how many acts there are, and where each act takes place.

There is often an introduction written by the director or producer, giving some background information about the particular piece, and perhaps providing some insight into how the rehearsal process resulted in certain staging decisions, or decisions about character portrayal. In addition most programmes will have a 'special thanks' section, crediting those people who have helped with the production in some capacity. Programmes are also often full of advertisements for other shows, restaurants, local businesses, etc. This is, of course, one very easy way of generating additional income for the production.

5 · Research and design

In the last chapter I described how the producer approaches various organisational aspects of the production once he or she has chosen a suitable show. While the producer is preoccupied with these concerns, the director and the other members of the creative team will be busy researching the show. This process is, to my mind, one of the many joys of directing a stage show, and this search for useful background material can often be both fascinating and inspiring.

Source texts

Many musicals are, of course, based upon existing works of literature, and the research process usually begins by getting thoroughly acquainted with the source text. Some examples of musicals which are based on well-known novels or plays are:

Leonard Bernstein's *West Side Story* (Shakespeare's *Romeo and Juliet*)
Lerner and Loewe's *My Fair Lady* (George Bernard Shaw's *Pygmalion*)
Lionel Bart's *Oliver!* (Charles Dickens' *Oliver Twist*)

Many other well-known musicals have origins which are somewhat more obscure. For example, Rodgers and Hammerstein's *Carousel* is based on the play *Liliom* by Hungarian playwright Ferenc Molnar, and Kander and Ebb's *Kiss of the Spiderwoman* is adapted from Manuel Puig's novel of the same name.

Reading the source text can be very illuminating, since it will inevitably provide detail which is impossible to incorporate into a normal length musical. Boublil and Schonberg's *Les Misérables*, for example, based on the lengthy French classic by Victor Hugo, is a very effective, but massively condensed version of the novel. Reading this original text is enormously useful in helping to flesh out the characters, and to provide a clear historical perspective on the piece as a whole.

As the director I will always try to read the source text and to become as familiar with it as possible, but it is not always easy to persuade the cast to do the same, especially if the source novel is long and complex, as is the case with *Les Misérables*. I recently directed an adaptation of Dickens' *David Copperfield*, a similarly long and detailed book, and while I encouraged the actors to read the novel, I also made notes as to where in the book the main character descriptions occur. So it was possible in the first few days of rehearsal to indicate clearly to the actors where to go to find out more about their individual characters. This may seem like spoon-feeding, perhaps, but it did at least ensure that each actor ended up with a very clear idea about Dickens' original intentions.

I often find that in the first few days of rehearsal, reference back to the source text can be a very good way of helping the cast to immerse themselves in the project. Perhaps I will ask the actors to read certain excerpts from the novel or play; perhaps we will use a scene from the original book to provide inspiration for an improvisation; or maybe we will look at other relevant passages from novels or poems by the same author. In this way the background material provides a good focal point, and I always find it to be of enormous help in kick-starting the rehearsal process. Even if the director ultimately decides to move away from the style or tone of the original work, I think that it is always important to know exactly what you are leaving behind.

Getting to know the show

When faced with the task of researching a specific show, some directors and choreographers will head straight to the video library to find an existing filmed version of the piece. There are, of course, many excellent films of well-known musicals – *Cabaret*, *Grease*, *The Sound of Music*, and *Little Shop of Horrors*, to name but a few. However, this approach can have its pitfalls. Apart from the fact that filmed musicals are often impossibly lavish and may be worlds away from anything that can be achieved on the stage, they are usually heavily adapted for the screen and can often differ enormously from the original script and score. *Cabaret* is a good example of this since the film includes several characters not featured in the stage show, and two of the key songs ('Money Makes the World go Around' and 'Maybe This Time') do not appear in the original musical score. Likewise, many directors have discovered to their surprise and dismay that the hit song 'Hopelessly Devoted to You' from *Grease* doesn't actually exist in the published score, but was written especially for the film. The licensing company will sometimes allow elements from the filmed version to be incorporated into the stage show, but there is no guarantee that this will be the case.

So, using videos can be a useful method of research, but it can also be a frustrating one. Some directors feel uncomfortable with this approach anyway, and prefer to come to the project with no preconceived visual ideas. Often more faithful to the original musical is the cast recording, and personally I find this a better way to become familiar with the score. A word of warning, though; by listening to a recording over and over again, it is very easy to become attached to the phrasing, the dynamics, and the tempos of that specific version. It is important to avoid this as far as possible and to remain flexible and open to new ideas, so that during rehearsals the actors are free to express themselves vocally and are not shoe-horned into recreating somebody else's work.

Getting to know the writers

The director will probably also want to find out something about the composer and lyricist of the show. This is easy with writers such as Richard Rodgers, Stephen Sondheim, or Leonard Bernstein, since there are scores of books which have been devoted to these major writers and their work. It is not so easy with lesser-known composers and lyricists, although there is usually some biographical material in CD booklets (assuming that the musical has been recorded), and old theatre programmes often yield some very interesting information also. Although they are few and far between, there are some shops that specialise in musical theatre, and in my experience they are often run by very enthusiastic and knowledgeable staff. A visit to one of these shops can save a lot of time in the search for appropriate background material (see appendix for a list of specialists).

While it is useful to know some biographical information about the writers, it is also helpful to know what other shows they wrote, when they were writing, and where in the canon of their work the particular musical being researched appears. Particularly with the more popular musicals, this kind of information can easily be gathered by doing a bit of selective reading, flicking through the odd biography, and, if access is available, searching on the Internet. There is also a new service available from Music Theatre International (see appendix) which provides video seminars on selected Broadway musicals such as *She Loves Me*, *Into the Woods*, *Assassins*, and *Annie*. These videos (called Video Conversation Pieces) bring together the various composers, lyricists, and performers involved in these selected Broadway productions, and between them they provide useful background information on the show, and offer advice on casting, characterisation, costume and set design.

Beyond the call of duty

I have worked on several musicals recently which have benefitted from some very detailed investigative work. Often, of course, there is not the time or money to do this sort of exhaustive research, but when there is, it can sometimes pay dividends. To prepare for a student production of a macabre musical retelling of the Jack the Ripper story (see photograph overleaf), I went on an organised London Walk, which covered the area of the East End where the late-nineteenth-century killings took place. The walk turned out to be both chilling and informative, and was, in fact, so useful in terms of background information that I took my students on the same walk a few weeks later.

I recently worked on a Japanese production of Rodgers and Hammerstein's *Carousel*, and for research purposes I was fortunate enough to get the chance to go to the coast of Maine to find out a bit about the setting of the piece, both social and geographical. Although this is a luxury which is not usually possible on any sort of theatrical project, the intimate knowledge I gained of the area, and of its

Five student actresses portray the ill-fated victims in Pember and de Marne's *Jack the Ripper* (PHOTO: Nick Davey)

quirks and customs, enabled me to help inspire a cast of Japanese actors in their performance of a musical which was as alien to them as a Kabuki performance would be to us.

The point is that research is not simply useful in determining how to stage a specific show; it is equally useful as a means of helping the actors to immerse themselves in the world of the piece.

Musical research

Just as it is important for the director to be well informed about the piece he or she is directing, so too is it a good idea for the musical director and the choreographer to do some groundwork before rehearsals begin. Some musical directors will go straight to a cast recording and study the piece from this. The hazards of doing so have already been mentioned however, and many musical directors will prefer to familiarise themselves with the piece by studying the score. He or she may also wish to listen to, or study, some other works by the same writers in order to get to grips with their particular style of writing. The musical director will also have to make some fairly early decisions about the instrumentation of the piece, and will need to find out what arrangements already exist, and whether they are suitable for the project in hand.

The choreographer will almost certainly want to listen to an existing recording of the piece, especially the danced sections of the show, and will want to get to know the music very well indeed, before he or she can start to think about how to stage or choreograph the numbers. The choreographer may also want to research a specific style of dance, such as the Jive (*Grease*), or the Tango (*Kiss of the Spiderwoman*), and he or she may need to consult specialist reference books, and watch specific dance videos to accomplish this.

Design research

As for the set designer, once preliminary discussions have taken place between the director and the design team, and once decisions have been made as to the period of the piece (and this may not necessarily correspond with previous productions of the same work), he or she can now start to think about a possible design for the show. This will usually involve some detailed research into the period, making special reference to style of architecture, type of furniture, and design and colour of fabrics. There are endless ways to research period detail, including reference books, works of literature, art galleries, museums and videos. It may well be the case that the finished design makes only a passing nod at authenticity, but even so, most designers will want to know something about the specific historical period before their creativity takes them off in a different direction.

The costume designer will usually approach research in a similar fashion, and very often the set designer and costume designer will research the piece together, since their work is so obviously interlinked. I recently worked on a production of *Oklahoma!* with a costume designer who was very keen to get away from the stereotypical gingham dresses that are so often associated with this particular musical. By consulting the appropriate reference books to determine the specific style of clothing worn in the American mid-West of the period, she then decided that all the women's skirts should be dyed in various shades of orange and yellow, and over-printed with a silhouette of corn sheaves. This inspired idea gave the production a very individual look which was both colourful and eye-catching. It was a decision which was also deeply rooted in the text, since throughout the show the lyrics continually refer to the natural beauty of the Oklahoma landscape. In our production, it was hardly an exaggeration to say that the corn was 'as high as an elephant's eye'.

As a director, I always try to ensure that every member of the creative team has access to a recording of the show and a copy of the libretto early on in the process. It is not enough for the set or costume designer to have 'a good idea what the piece is all about'. He or she must be familiar with the specific details of the show before being able to design an effective set or appropriate costumes.

Creative teamwork

Once each member of the creative team has had the opportunity to do some individual research, more specific design ideas will start to take shape. At this stage there will usually be a meeting between the director and the design team (set, costume, and sometimes lighting). Obviously there is no fixed agenda at a creative meeting of this sort, but often the set designer will have done some preliminary sketches, and the costume designer may well have brought along some suitable costume illustrations and perhaps some fabric samples too. This meeting should provide a good opportunity for everyone to express their ideas about the production before any specific 'concept' has been defined. It is important, though, however stimulating the design ideas may be, for the director to remember that ultimately the show is about a group of characters telling a particular story. The set and costume designs must facilitate this story-telling, and not simply provide a beautiful but lifeless piece of window-dressing. It seems a very obvious thing to say, but in my experience designers can get so caught up in the style of their design, that they forget that it has to function as a practical set, and it is there to enhance the actors' performances, not to detract from them.

As a director, I love the process involved in creating a visual identity for a production, and I find the preliminary design discussions stimulating and exciting. However, I always try to keep in mind two basic questions: will the design fulfil the practical needs of the show? – i.e., can each scene be successfully played out within this design concept?; and does the design help or hinder the story-telling?

Trends in theatre design have changed enormously over the last few decades. In the past audiences expected huge scenic changes to occur between each act or even each scene of a stage musical, and scenery was often elaborate and detailed. The current trend is for something simpler, more abstract, and less obviously representational. In the contemporary theatre, more often than not, the separate acts of a musical will take place within the same basic framework; the look of each scene may be varied by introducing scenic trucks, by flying in extra bits of set, or by revolving the stage to create a new perspective, but there is essentially a unified feel to the whole design. Modern audiences are less willing to sit in the dark for five minutes while an elaborate set change is in progress, and often scene changes, such as they are, occur in full view of the audience, and even in some cases become incorporated into the action of a scene. The modern audience has, if you like, learned to accept that a single branch hanging from the sky can represent a tree, or indeed a whole forest; it can accept minimal visual clues and allow imagination to make up the rest of the picture.

This minimal approach is not, of course, something exclusive to contemporary theatre, in fact the audience was required to do the same sort of 'imaginative leaping' during Shakespeare's time, when theatres such as The Globe offered very little in the way of scenery.

Just as the modern set often has a basic unified design, costume designs in musical theatre are often simplified, usually to give each character a strong visual identity, often to facilitate movement, and sometimes purely for financial reasons. The audience very quickly accepts the convention that a character's basic costume can be added to as the story develops, rather than changed entirely from scene to scene. Hence it is not unusual for the heroine to be wearing the same dress in Act I and Act II of the show, even if there is a time difference of weeks or even months.

I am not trying to pretend that modern productions are all done in a pared down, more economical fashion. This is clearly not the case with shows like *The Phantom of the Opera* and *Miss Saigon*. I am merely referring to a general shift in attitude, and there are always going to be exceptions to any rule, especially in an area such as the theatre where rules are made to be broken.

The design meeting

During the preliminary design discussions, various questions will need to be addressed:

How should the available performance space be used? If the theatre is a flexible space, the director and designers will need to decide how to use it to its best advantage. Should the theatre be used in-the-round, for example, with the audience surrounding the actors? Or should there be a thrust stage whereby the acting space extends out into the audience? These decisions will depend upon the nature of show that is being presented, the size and flexibility of the stage, and the type of actor-audience relationship required by the director.

Where will the orchestra or band be seated, and how will the conductor communicate with the actors on stage? Since musicals always require some sort of instrumental accompaniment, these are very important issues to address. In some cases these decisions will affect the sound designer and he or she should be contacted at an early stage if this is the case. If, for example, the band and conductor are placed at the back of the stage, it may be necessary to amplify them, both for the sake of the audience, and for the actors on stage. If, on the other hand, the musicians are to be placed on stage in full view of the audience, how will this affect the 'look' of the show? Will the lights on their music stands affect the overall lighting on stage? Will the musicians need to be costumed to remain in keeping with the style of the show? If so, this will inevitably affect the costume budget, so any decisions of this sort need to be very carefully considered, and at an early stage.

How many actors will be on stage at any one time? The overall design for the show will, of course, be affected by the number of performers on stage. If the show requires a large ensemble, or if there are to be big ensemble dance numbers, the designer will need to be aware of this and will usually try to avoid cluttering up the set unnecessarily. On the other hand, if the cast is fairly small, and the performers are doubling or tripling parts, the designer may decide that a busy set actually makes the actors look less isolated and helps to create a more interesting stage picture.

How can scene changes be incorporated, and how can they be achieved as quickly and effectively as possible? Obviously one of the main challenges facing the set designer is how to change the set to accommodate each separate scene. Some shows are particularly problematic as far as this is concerned. The scenic descriptions for *Carousel*, for example, are as follows: an amusement park; a path along the shore; Nettie's spa; an island off the coast; the docks; 'up there' (i.e., purgatory); outside Julie's cottage sixteen years later; and outside a schoolhouse. Somehow the designer for this show needs to find a way of creating these very varied locations without interrupting the flow of the piece. Sometimes the designer will decide that the necessary location change can be achieved by a dramatic change of lighting, rather than any particular change in the set. If this is the case then the lighting designer should certainly participate in these early design discussions.

What is the nature of the movement in the show, and how will this affect the costumes? This is a question which needs to be addressed at an early stage since it will have an impact on the way that the costume designer approaches his or her work. If the piece is a heavy dance show like *West Side Story*, *On Your Toes*, or *Crazy For You*, clearly the costumes will need to be specially designed to accommodate this, and the material used for costumes will need to have more flexibility than that used for non-dancing shows. Dance footwear will also be a top priority.

Are there any quick changes in the show? The costume designer must make sure that any quick changes that occur in the musical are aided, not hampered by the costume design. There is no point in dressing someone in lace-up ankle boots if the actor has just twenty seconds to change into something else. If these problems are addressed from the outset, valuable time, not to mention money, can be saved, and last-minute panics avoided.

Clearly these early design meetings are not just about throwing around creative ideas; they are also about facing some of the practicalities of staging the show, and trying to find possible solutions to a whole range of different problems.

Finalising designs

The next stage is to commit to a specific design idea or concept for the show. By concept I am not necessarily implying a radical reworking of the piece; I am really referring to a through line in terms of staging and design. For example, the recent Broadway production of Cy Coleman's *City of Angels* used a simple, but very effective device for telling the story. For the 'real life' scenes, the sets, costumes and props, were designed in glorious technicolour, while the movie scenes were all limited to various shades of black and white. This was not only extremely striking visually, but it also helped to make the story very clear. For a recent production of Stephen Sondheim's *Into the Woods* which I directed, we used a very simple concept to create a striking stage design. Everything was based on the idea of the forest, and the set consisted of a huge spiral walkway with trees growing through it. Above the platform were the large trunks of several trees, and below it were the tangled, knotted roots of the forest's underbelly. This design explored in visual terms one of the major themes of the piece; it mirrored the idea that uncomfortable truths which in life usually lie hidden are in this musical cruelly exposed.

Set sketch by designer Graham Wynne for *Into the Woods*

As far as costume was concerned for this production of *Into the Woods*, we decided that since the story features a collection of well-known characters from an assortment of different fairytales, we would make sure that these characters were instantly recognisable as soon as they set foot on the stage. The costume designer, by sifting through numerous illustrated books of fairytales, created a series of designs which gave each of the characters a 'classic' look, and which helped to bring these familiar story-book figures to life.

Two illustrations by costume designer Charlotte Sewell for *Into the Woods*

The model box

Once the concept has been decided upon and agreed by the design team, the set designer will concentrate on refining his or her ideas, and will usually construct a scaled-down model of the set. This is called the model box (see page 57). Ideally the model box should be completed several weeks before rehearsals begin, giving the set designer a chance to see how the set will look in reality, and allowing the director the opportunity to suggest alterations if necessary.

Lighting and sound

Once the model box is completed, the lighting designer will have a much clearer idea about how to approach the lighting for the show. Although he or she may well have been involved in preliminary meetings and discussed various ideas with the director and designer, it is only now that the lighting designer can really start to make concrete plans. At this stage in the process the set designer and lighting designer will need to discuss the practicalities of the set, and to work out how best to light the stage area, and from which lighting positions. The sound designer (if required on the project) will also need to see the model at this stage, in order to start thinking about how best to amplify the show, and where to place fold-back speakers, etc.

The costume plan

Often by this stage the costume designer will have a fairly clear idea how to go about costuming the show, and may have prepared a set of illustrations for the director to have a look at (see the examples from *Into the Woods* on page 42). Of course it is practically impossible to be certain about any costume design until the designer has met the actors and has taken note of their physical types, colour of hair etc. But having a basic costume plan to work from is certainly a bonus, even if things change dramatically during rehearsals as the costume designer gets to know the actors better, and as the actors get to grips with their roles and start to have an opinion about what their characters would and would not wear.

In the best of all possible situations the costume designer will finalise costume designs fairly late in the process, since it is then possible to design outfits around the specific actors in the show. In practice, however, this luxury is not often a viable one since rehearsal periods are usually fairly short, and all the costumes need to be finished if not by the first full run-through, then certainly by the first dress rehearsal. If the costumes are being hired, however, it is often possible to make final decisions later in rehearsals, since in this situation the time-consuming process of actually making the costumes is not an issue.

While on the subject of costumes, it is important to remember that most musicals will place a greater emphasis upon movement than straight plays. Costumes must therefore be designed to accommodate this, and footwear in particular must be high on the costume designer's list of priorities. For *Carousel* the dancers were supplied with split-soled jazz boots for the rigorous dance numbers, and a more 'period' alternative for the non-dancing scenes. While the costume design required that the womens' skirts were layered with petticoats, in practice it was discovered that the extra weight caused significant problems during the dance sections and a thinner, more light-weight material was subsequently provided as a workable alternative.

Clearly it is wise for the costume designer and the choreographer to liaise before the finished designs are presented to the company. Communication between these two departments at this stage can prevent time and money being wasted on costumes which, while aesthetically pleasing, may be impossible to wear within the context of the show.

Building the set

In normal circumstances once the model box has been approved by the director, the set can start to be built. It is vital that the model is to scale since the set builders will be using it as a template for their work. In addition to the model box there will usually be a ground plan which gives detailed information about the exact dimensions of the set.

It is important to remember that the process of putting on a musical is one which involves experimentation and discovery. Once in the rehearsal room, ideas develop or change altogether, and the director and his design team must be responsive to this. Some decisions, of course, will have to be made before rehearsals begin, and in most cases, much of the set design will have to be finalised fairly early on so that there is adequate time for building and painting. But where possible, costume designs, lighting plots and prop designs should not be set in stone before the director has had time to work with the actors in the rehearsal room. It is a good idea to continue to have design meetings during the rehearsal period, so that adjustments can be made as the piece develops. A production that is aleady fixed in terms of set, costume, and lighting design, before the actors have even set foot in the rehearsal room, may be a competent piece of entertainment, but is never going to be a thrilling piece of theatre.

6 · Casting the show

Auditions can be an exciting and often unnerving experience, not only for the auditionees, but also for the audition panel. Having already invested a large amount of time and energy in the production, the director, producer, musical director, and choreographer will be quietly praying that the right people walk through the audition room door. After all, what is the point of putting on a production of *Cabaret*, for example, without a stunning performer to play Sally Bowles? Likewise a production of *The King and I* without a charismatic king at its centre is never really going to take off. So, it is most important that auditions are well publicised in order that the audition panel has a wide choice of options when casting the show.

If the production is a school or community project, then it is most likely that the director will have some idea about who will be attending the auditions. With productions of this sort, which usually have a specific pool of potential performers, publicising auditions is usually done through notice-boards, bulletins, and local newspapers. If the production is a professional, or semi-professional one, on the other hand, the director may not know who will be attending auditions, and in such circumstances it is crucial that the auditions are well publicised. This can be achieved in a variety of different ways:

- By placing advertisements in newspapers, such as *The Stage* (see appendix).

- By contacting theatrical agents directly and supplying them with a character breakdown for the show (a list of agents can be found in *Contacts* - see appendix).

- By placing casting breakdowns in theatrical bulletins such as SBS or PCR (see appendix).

- By using the services of a casting agent who will contact agents directly and draw up suitable audition lists.

The casting breakdown for a specific show should not only give a clear idea about the type of actor required for each role, but should also specify the special skills required for the part, such as dance ability, acting skills, and vocal range. For an example of a cast breakdown for some of the principal roles in Rodgers and Hammerstein's *Carousel* see overleaf.

Character breakdown for Carousel

(for some of the principal characters only)

BILLY BIGELOW   Vocal range: bottom B flat to top G
                     Age: mid 20s to mid 30s

Billy is a carousel barker working at the fairground. He is tall, good-looking, tough and proud. Although he is imposing and confident, he is a complicated mixture of aggression and sensitivity, and occasionally shows a tenderness which seems at odds with his general character.

JULIE JORDAN   Vocal range: middle C to top G flat
                     Age: late teens to early 20s

Julie is a young, attractive girl who works at the local mill. She is a loner and a dreamer, and likes to keep herself to herself. Like Billy she has a restless but sensitive nature.

NETTIE FOWLER   Vocal range: middle C to top G
                     Age: not specified, although she should probably be late 30s to late 50s.

Nettie is a warm-hearted, generous woman who acts as a surrogate aunt to all the young villagers. She has a wisdom and experience which the younger characters lack, but she also has a great sense of fun.

JIGGER   Vocal range: D (below middle C) to B (below middle C). NB vocal ability not important.
              Age: not specified, but he should probably be late 20s to late 30s, although he could be older.

Jigger is the villain of the piece. He is a sailor who works on a whaling ship, and he is rough, sinister, and unscrupulous. He also has a mischievous sense of humour and enjoys flirting with the girls.

LOUISE   Vocal range: Non-singing role
              Age: 16

Louise is the daughter of Billy and Julie (she appears only in the second half of the show when the action jumps forward by a number of years). Although she is not required to sing, she must be a very accomplished dancer, preferably ballet-trained. Like her parents she has a restless spirit, and although she comes across as tough and strong-minded, there is vulnerability about her too.

When to hold auditions?
This is a difficult question to answer since it will vary enormously according to the specific circumstances of the production. For some big, commercial shows, casting is done months in advance, but in most situations, it is done much closer to the start of the rehearsal period. It is not unknown for the production team to be auditioning actors several days before rehearsals begin. Although producers may often be very keen to make casting decisions fairly early on, many actors are unwilling to commit themselves to a project too far in advance. In my experience, casting about a month prior to rehearsals makes life easier for everyone. It is certainly useful for the costume designer, since he or she can get measurements in good time and see what the cast is going to look like before the first day of rehearsals.

Setting up auditions
The producer, often with the help of the stage manager, will usually be in charge of organising auditions. The first thing to do is to select a suitable audition venue. In the case of school or college productions, this is not normally a problem, but in a situation where rooms are not readily available, finding the right audition space can be time-consuming and expensive. It is always best to check audition rooms in person before booking them, since in my experience they can often be quite unsuitable.

The most important aspect of a rehearsal space is that it is big enough for your purposes. If the show has a strong dance element, for example, the choreographer will need to see the dancers in action, and it will be most frustrating if they can only be seen in small groups due to a chronic lack of space. Some choreographers may also prefer that the room has a mirrored wall, so that the dancers can see themselves as they learn the audition choreography. There will also need to be a piano in the room, and this piano should be checked to see that it is in tune. It is not only the auditioning actors who will suffer from an out-of-tune keyboard; the panel will soon lose their sense of humour if forced to listen to a string of atonal audition songs.

Ideally an audition room should be well sound-proofed, so that noise from adjoining rooms does not interfer with the audition process. It is also very useful to have another room, or an anti-chamber, where the auditionees can sit and wait (or read a section of the script) before being called in for their audition. Since auditions often do not run to schedule, it can get very uncomfortable if there is nowhere for the auditionees to go while waiting for their call.

The audition

Auditions come in all shapes and sizes; from an informal chat in someone's front room, to a terrifying open audition on the stage of a huge West End playhouse. Every director will have a slightly different approach to casting, but although audition procedure may vary from show to show, every audition panel will have the same basic objective; to find the best possible cast for the production. And this does not simply mean selecting a group of highly talented individuals – it means choosing a team of performers who will work *together* to present the best possible interpretation of the piece. The director is not simply looking for the most talented performers for the job, he or she will also be looking to select a company of actors who will work as a team.

The audition panel

In most cases the audition panel will include the director, the musical director, and the producer. For musicals which involve complicated movement there will usually be a choreographer present, and in auditions for large-scale commercial musicals the panel can expand to include a casting director, several assistants, a stage manager, and an orchestral arranger.

Other personnel involved in the audition usually include several members of stage management (to usher performers into the audition room, and to organise scripts and music) and, most importantly, the audition pianist. Sometimes the musical director will act as the accompanist, but this is not an ideal situation since he or she will want to concentrate on listening to the performers' voices rather than struggling to play a difficult piano accompaniment. Audition accompanists must, above all else, be excellent sight-readers, since they will be expected to play by sight any song that the audition candidates bring with them. They will certainly need to be familiar with the music from the specific show being cast, and they may also be called upon to transpose songs at sight into different keys. It is vitally important to find a good audition accompanist, and this should be a priority for anyone involved in organising musical auditions.

Open auditions

Auditions which are open to anyone wishing to attend are not surprisingly known as 'open auditions'. They are usually, although not exclusively, used for casting commercial musicals or big dance shows, and they are often very well attended. Although they can be anti-climatic and soul-destroying from the point-of-view of the auditionee, who may have to wait two or three hours before being manoeuvred on to the stage, allowed to sing half a song, and then ushered back into the wings, this procedure does enable a large number of candidates to be seen in a relatively short space of time. However this impersonal means of selecting potential cast members is somewhat old-fashioned, and thankfully seems to be the exception rather than the rule in contemporary theatre.

Private auditions

A much better procedure, to my mind, is the closed private audition, where performers will be given a specific audition time, and will usually get the chance to meet and talk with the audition panel. This approach has many benefits; not least that the auditionee is usually given a greater opportunity to show what he or she can do. Also, the audition panel is able to get a much stronger impression of the audition candidate, not only in terms of his or her acting and singing ability, but also with regard to personality.

Under normal circumstances, the auditionees will be expected to bring several songs of their choice to the audition, and they will be encouraged to bring music which is stylistically similar to the show being cast. For example, an audition candidate for Kander and Ebb's *Chicago* might bring two contrasting songs from several other shows by the same writers, such as *Kiss of the Spiderwoman*, *The Rink*, or *Cabaret*. In some cases, especially where principal roles are being cast, the actors will have been sent specific music from the show. They will be expected to learn this music and to come to the audition prepared to sing it. They may also receive a section of the script before the audition, and they will be expected to be familiar with this also.

Once in the audition room, anything can happen; it all depends upon the type of show being cast, and the casting procedure favoured by the director. However, the auditionee will usually be asked to sing, often required to read, and sometimes asked to dance (or required to return for a dance audition at a later date). Some directors will also ask the actor to improvise, although in my experience this is fairly rare. As a director, I find that a good way of starting the audition is to sit the actor down, introduce myself and the other members of the team, and then have a fairly informal chat about the nature of the production, and the sort of performers that we are looking to cast. I may also ask some questions about the actor's recent theatrical experience. This is particularly useful when an actor or an actor's agent has not provided a curriculum vitae (CV). With most professional productions, a CV and a recent photo will have been provided by the agent prior to the audition, but with amateur or semi-professional shows the actor is usually required to fill in a form before entering the audition room to provide relevant details about past theatrical productions. The purpose of this informal chat is fairly self-evident; most importantly it helps to relax the actor before he or she has to perform, but it also provides the panel with an opportunity to get to know the actor, and to start to assess how well he or she may fit into the company.

Classifying the audition candidates

One of the biggest problems when casting a musical, especially if there are large numbers auditioning for the show, is how to remember each auditionee, and how to compare them with other candidates who may have auditioned on a different day, or even on a different week. I usually try to use a basic classification system for each of the different disciplines, which goes from A for very good, to C for poor, with pluses and minuses to help the differentiation. Obviously this is a fairly crude method, but it does at least provide some means of comparison. I also try to take fairly detailed notes while the actors are auditioning, not only concerning their performance ability, but also referring to their physical characteristics, and what they are wearing. Basically, I find that it is worth noting anything which may help to recall a particular actor, especially if auditions are spaced out over a period of weeks. These notes can also come in very handy for future productions, since an actor who is perhaps not suitable for one show may be perfect for another.

Recalls

Most directors will expect to hold recalls once the first set of auditions has taken place. For these, the selected actors may be sent specific sections of music or script to learn, and they will almost certainly be expected to read and sing something from the show during their recall (this may not always be the case with prospective ensemble members who are unlikely to be featured in the show in a solo capacity). When drawing up the recall lists, the stage management should try to ensure that each candidate is given a reasonable amount of time for his or her audition. Ten or fifteen minutes is often adequate, but it will, of course, depend on the type of show, and the role that is being auditioned for. It is a good idea, when organising the audition list, to add the occasional fifteen minutes of catch-up time, so that if one audition overruns it doesn't necessarily mean that the rest of the day's auditions are delayed.

From the point of view of the audition panel, recalls can be absolutely invaluable since there is usually more time to work with the actors, and a greater opportunity to assess their individual talents. It is also possible, and most profitable, to get certain actors to perform scenes together to discover how well they complement each other. For example, for a production of *Oklahoma!* the director might wish to see how a prospective Curly and a prospective Laurey work together. If there is clearly no chemistry between the two actors, the central relationship in the show will be seriously undermined, and the director should therefore try auditioning the couple with different partners. It is often useful at the recall stage to have an actor on hand to read in extra parts, if necessary. This can, of course, be done by one of the production team, but it is better all round if a spare actor can be found to do it, since the auditionee will usually respond better to reading with a fellow actor, and the audition panel will then be free to concentrate on observing the scene, rather than participating in it.

While recalls are an integral and extremely valuable part of the whole casting process, directors should try to limit the number of recalls that they require any one actor to attend, since it is taking unfair advantage of the auditionee to expect him or her to return six or seven times. I strongly believe that if a production team cannot make up their minds having seen the performer two or three times, then this probably indicates that the candidate is not ideal for the production.

Dance auditions

The nature of the dance audition will very much depend upon the dance requirements of the show. If the musical is basically a dance show, such as *A Chorus Line* or *42nd Street*, then the dance auditions will become a major priority, and will probably be attended by the entire production team. If, however, the dancing in the show is secondary, and the actors are required to 'move' rather than dance, then the dance auditions will be of less importance, and can be carried out by the choreographer independently. He or she can then discuss the dance ability of each performer with the director and musical director before any firm decisions are made about casting. It is worth mentioning that actors should always be warned in advance if it is likely that they will have to do any dancing or movement during the audition, so that they can then dress accordingly. Not only is it difficult for the panel to assess someone's dancing ability if she is wearing a tight pencil skirt, or a pair of heavy boots, it is also embarrassing for the auditionee.

Five 'Gentlemen of Japan' from *Hot Mikado* (PHOTO: Nick Davey)

Checklist for auditions

As I have said, auditions vary according to the needs of the show, and the personalities of the production team. For this reason I have not gone into minute detail about what actually goes on in the audition room, since every director, choreographer, and musical director will have a different approach. However, during the course of the auditions and recalls, it is important to make sure that the following points are covered (this list refers to a show in which the actors are all expected to sing, dance, and act):

- What is the vocal range of the auditionee? Does the voice suit the musical style of the show? Is it a strong, resiliant voice? (This is particularly relevant if the show is likely to have a long run).
- What is the dance ability of the audition candidate? What are his or her specific strengths – jazz, ballet, contemporary, or tap? Does his or her dancing style suit the choreographic language of the show?
- What is the acting ability of the auditionee? Does he or she have good diction? Is he or she good at accents?
- Does the auditionee have any useful special skills, such as juggling, acrobatics, fire-eating, playing musical instruments, etc?

- What is the availability of the audition candidate? Is he or she free to attend all the rehearsals and performances?

- If cast in the show, would the auditionee accept an ensemble part, an understudy, or only a principal role?

- Will the audition candidate fit in with the team and be a good company member?

Finalising casting

Making the final decisions on casting can be an agonising part of the process, and in my experience it is seldom that a production team will be in absolute agreement about who to choose. Often the choreographer will favour one person because of his or her particular dance ability, while the musical director may feel that another performer is vocally perfect for the show. The director, on the other hand, may dismiss both these candidates because of a perceived lack of acting ability. Of course, it is absolutely impossible to please everyone, and there are bound to be some disagreements at this stage. Ultimately it is the director who must have the final word on casting, but he or she must be very careful to listen to the advice of the other members of the team. If a part is specifically intended for a dancer, such as the Carnival Boy in *Carousel*, for example, then the director should be strongly advised by the choreographer. Similarly, if the part requires an exceptional singer, such as Cunégonde in *Candide*, then the director will need to listen carefully to the advice of the musical director.

Often the casting of principal roles is fairly clear-cut, and assuming that the actors have all been through the recall stage, the production team will usually have a fairly good idea of a specific actor's suitability for a particular part. Often more problematic, in terms of casting, is the ensemble. The reason for this is simple; an ensemble member is often required to be a good all-rounder; i.e. good at singing, dancing, and acting. On top of this he or she may be required to understudy a principal role. Inevitably members of the production team are likely to favour the candidate who is strongest in their particular discipline, but for the good of the production, a certain amount of compromise may be necessary at this stage. This is often achieved by 'trading hostages'; for example, the choreographer may agree to the casting of a less talented dancer so that the musical director can have a superb high tenor in the ensemble, on the understanding that an excellent dancer who may be less vocally talented will also be cast in the show.

Although it is unusual for school, college, or community productions to allocate understudies for principal roles, for most commercial shows it is a necessity. In such cases the priority when casting the ensemble is to find performers with the specific talents to understudy the principal parts. This inevitably adds to the already complicated process of casting the ensemble.

Making offers

Once the casting has been finalised, the actors will need to be notified as soon as possible. With in-house productions at a school or college, this is often done by placing a cast list on one of the main notice-boards. With professional productions the actors will usually be notified through their agents, and in the absence of an agent, they will be called at home.

At this stage in the casting process, there are several important things to remember. Firstly, an actor who has been selected for the show may decide to turn the job down. Maybe a better offer has already been received, or perhaps he or she has decided against committing themselves to this particular project. It is always wise to have a contingency plan as far as casting is concerned, and this means compiling a list of actors who would be the second preference for casting in the show. Clearly it is unwise to let these people know that they haven't been chosen until the first preference cast have all accepted their roles.

Once the offers have been accepted, however, it is important to let the unsuccessful actors know that they have not been cast in the show. Far too many producers simply fail to notify actors about their casting decisions, even if these actors have learned specific sections of music and script from the show, and have attended numerous recalls. This, to my mind, is simply thoughtless and disrespectful. Of course, in the case of a big musical, where large numbers of performers are being auditioned, it may not be practical to inform every single person about final casting decisions. My own particular belief is that if an actor has been *recalled* for a particular project, then he or she should be informed, either through the agent, by letter, or by telephone. If an actor can be bothered to make the considerable effort to attend a recall, having learned sections of music and script, then he or she should at least be given the courtesy of a response.

Which brings me to an important point about casting; respect for the actors. It is all too easy to get swept up in the whole process of casting, and to forget that the numerous actors auditioning for the show are basically just vulnerable individuals hoping to be chosen for a role. No matter how experienced an actor may be, auditioning can still be a nerve-wracking experience. It is important that the production team recognise this, and treat each auditionee with courtesy and respect. The archetypal director who sits in a darkened auditorium and yells 'next!' as soon as an audition candidate begins to sing, should, to my mind, be drummed out of the theatre. Putting an actor in an uncomfortable, and potentially humiliating position is not only disrespectful, it is also hardly likely to result in a good audition, which is, after all, the whole point of the procedure.

Once final casting decisions have been made, it is important to make sure that the actors who have been chosen do not change their 'look' in any significant way before rehearsals begin, unless they have been specifically requested to do so by the director. This applies to beards and moustaches, and hairstyles in general, particularly with reference to hair colour. The cast should be encouraged to check with the director before making any significant changes to their appearance.

Casting children

A brief word about casting children in theatrical productions. Some musicals, such as *Bugsy Malone*, and *Oliver!*, require a large number of children in the cast. There are strict guidelines concerning the appearance of children on stage, and it is important before organising auditions to ascertain what rules and regulations apply in the specific area where the production is to take place. The producer should contact his or her local authority for details.

Children under a certain age are only permitted to appear in a limited number of performances per year, and it is therefore often necessary when casting a show to double or triple-cast these parts. There are also other issues to take into consideration such as performance times and chaperone requirements which must be addressed if children are to be used in the production. Discipline is also sometimes a problem with child performers, and for this reason it is important during the casting process to try to choose children who have a good

An 'angel' from the Tokyo production of *Carousel*, originally produced at the Royal National Theatre, and originally directed by Nicholas Hytner (PHOTO: Toho Co. Ltd)

attention span, and who are unlikely to be disruptive. Since they will inevitably spend much of their time hanging around waiting to rehearse or perform, they will need to be well disciplined. The theatre is potentially a very dangerous place, and the director will want to avoid having a bunch of unruly children rampaging through the wings, no matter how talented they may be as performers.

It is of prime importance where children are concerned that the director should be well organised, since in my experience the type of experimentation which works well with adult actors is not always appropriate for younger performers. I try to plan rehearsals very carefully if children are involved, so that I can give clear instructions when it comes to staging a scene or song. Children do not respond well to indecisiveness and as soon as a director starts to deliberate for any length of time their attention tends to wander and the rehearsal loses its focus.

It may seem an obvious point to make, but it is important to remember to give children regular breaks during rehearsals. This can be beneficial not only to the children, but also to the production team, since controlling a room full of enthusiastic young performers can be an exhausting experience. Several well-timed breaks will give both children and adults the opportunity to recharge their batteries.

7 · The first day of rehearsals

Having been on both sides of the production desk, as a director and an actor, I can say with some authority that the first day of rehearsals is always a nerve-wracking experience for all concerned. Everyone is anxious to make a good impression, the director is praying for the day to go smoothly, the designer is concerned about showing his or her set designs, the whole production team are hoping that they have cast the right set of performers for the job, and the actors are worried about the impression they'll make on their fellow actors. In short, the room will be buzzing with nervous energy.

Every director will have his or her own way of structuring the first day, and it would be foolish to suggest that there is any set way of going about this. There are, however, certain ways of making this important first day more productive for all concerned, and this is what I shall be hoping to demonstrate in this chapter.

Coffee and tea are always good ice-breakers, and it is not a bad idea to start proceedings with a drink and an informal chat, so that everyone can meet everyone else, gossip with old friends, and work off some excess nervous energy. If possible, the director and the other members of the production team should try to make sure that they know everyone's name at this early stage in rehearsals, so that introductions can easily be made without referring to lists. Not only does this preparatory name-learning help to save time in rehearsals, it also makes the actors feel much more welcome and helps to establish them as an important part of the company, regardless of their particular role in the show. There is nothing worse than a director who spends all the time chatting up the principals, but clearly hasn't a clue who the ensemble members are. It is a fairly obvious point to make, but an actor who feels like a valued member of the cast is bound to invest more emotional energy in the project as a whole.

Once the company members have had a chance to meet each other and chat informally, the stage management will usually take their cue from the director and assemble the company. With larger numbers of people it is best to set out chairs in a circle so that everyone can see everyone else. A circle is, after all, the perfect democratic shape, since everyone is as important as the next person. It is good to steer away from any sense of hierarchy at this early stage in rehearsals (such as principals at the front, ensemble at the back) and a circular seating plan helps to avoid this problem.

The producer should try to ensure that the whole company is present at this preliminary discussion; the actors, the stage management, the director, the choreographer, the musical director, the designer, the costume designer, the lighting designer, the sound designer, the rehearsal pianist, and any assistants to the various members of the production team. On larger productions there may also be a production manager, production assistants, and a representative from the publicity department.

Introductions

Once everyone is seated it is usually a good idea to get everyone to introduce themselves, even if most people have already met up during the informal coffee break. Not only does this help to ensure that everyone is properly introduced, it also gives each actor the chance to speak at a very early point in rehearsals. It may seem a strange thing to say, but not all actors are confident and outgoing, and some, if given half a chance, will fade into the background at the earliest opportunity. I believe it to be very important that everyone feels that they have a contribution to make to the production, and the sooner the actors realise that they are allowed to 'have a voice' in rehearsals, the better.

Once these introductions have been made, I usually try to give the cast some background information about the production itself. This may include details about the show's history, some information about the writers, and reviews from

A church in New England (PHOTO: Matthew White)

previous productions. I will always try to give the show some sort of context, and if the musical is derived from a well-known source, as is the case with *Oliver!* or *Candide*, I may read some excerpts from the original text, or discuss the source material in general terms.

Photographs can also be useful during these introductory talks, and I recently found, when introducing *Carousel*, that some pictures which I had taken on my visit to the coast of Maine provided a very useful reference point during early discussions with the cast. One picture (see opposite) gave a very clear impression of the architectural style of a typical New England church – a style which provided the inspiration for some stunning set designs for our production. The cast were also interested to see pictures of the unique Maine coastline, dotted with thousands of tiny islands, one such island being the focus for the famous clambake in Act II of the musical.

The model box

The model box is the clearest, most accurate means of indicating how the final stage designs will look in the theatre. It is usually on a scale of half an inch to a foot (1:25 cm), and is made to look as much like the finished stage design as possible (see overleaf). The set designer will usually want to present the model box to the cast on the first day of rehearsals. This can be a very exciting and theatrical moment for the actors, who will probably, up to this point, have very little idea about how the show is going to look. Since this is the first time that the set design is actually revealed to the cast, it is best not to pre-empt the moment by leaving the model box uncovered in the rehearsal room from the start of the day.

The set designer, sometimes with the assistance of the director, will usually want to talk through the various sets, showing how scene changes will be achieved throughout the course of the show. Once this has been done, the cast should be given ample opportunity to question the designer about any aspect of the set which is unclear. The model box will usually be left in the rehearsal room for the rest of the day so that the cast members can familiarise themselves with it at their leisure. It will then be returned to the workshop so that work can continue on building the set. In the case of some school or college productions, the designer may not feel it necessary to provide a detailed model of the set, particularly if the design is very simple. In such cases, he or she should try to provide some drawings, at the very least, so that the cast will have some idea of the nature of the set that they will be working on.

Once the model box has been presented, the costume designer may wish to show the cast some costume sketches (see p. 42) and talk to them about basic design ideas. And while the whole cast is gathered together under one roof, the costume designer may wish to check the actors' measurements and note down any that have not already been submitted. (These measurements are usually provided before the rehearsals begin, either by the actors' agents, or by the actors themselves.)

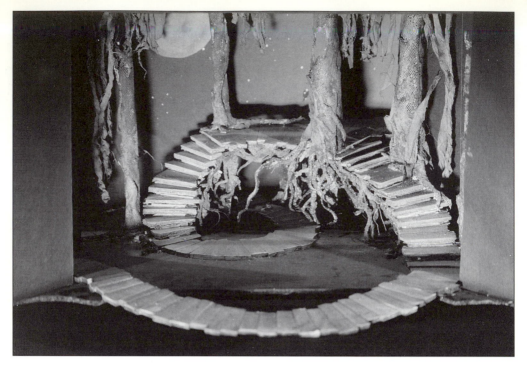

The model box for Sondheim's *Into the Woods* (PHOTO: Dan Hill)

Input from the producer and the stage manager

The producer will also probably want to talk to the cast at some stage during the day. If the poster and flyers for the production have already been printed, it is a very good idea for the producer to distribute some of these to the cast as soon as possible. He or she may also wish to discuss other aspects of publicity, such as prospective photo calls, radio interviews and other media events.

The presence of the stage manager is also vital on the first day. The job of stage manager is, as described in Chapter 3, a demanding one, and he or she will need to establish themselves as an authoritative individual early on in the rehearsal process. Also it is important that the actors know who to turn to should they require any practical help. The relationship between the performers and the stage management team is a crucial one, since they will be working closely together throughout the rehearsal period, and indeed throughout the whole run. It is very important to start to establish a rapport as early as possible.

The stage management will usually compile a contact sheet and distribute it on the first day of rehearsals. The contact sheet is a comprehensive list which provides addresses and contact numbers for everyone involved in the production. The actors will need to know who to contact if for any reason they are unable to make a rehearsal, and this should be clearly indicated on the sheet. The cast will also need to know where to look for their rehearsal calls; there will usually be a notice-board in or near the rehearsal room that can be used for this purpose. It is also worth the stage manager pointing out at this early stage that rehearsal clothes should be worn to all rehearsals unless otherwise stated (sometimes the director will advise a particular actor to wear clothes to rehearsals which reflect the role he or she is playing, in order to help get a general feel for the character). Rehearsal clothes should be informal and comfortable, and scruffy enough for the actors to feel entirely at ease in rehearsals without worrying about damaging their outfits. If dancing is involved in the show, the performers should probably check with the choreographer about rehearsal footwear.

The stage manager may also wish to lay down one or two basic ground rules before rehearsals begin in earnest. In my experience actors are not normally permitted to smoke in the rehearsal rooms, especially in musical productions where singing is of paramount importance. The stage manager needs to stress this right from the start of rehearsals, and if possible should let the actors know which parts of the building have been designated as smoking areas. Likewise, the stage manager may wish to ban bags and coats from the rehearsal room, since they can often interfere with the rehearsal process, providing a constant source of distraction in the shape of chewing gum, newspapers, and most especially mobile phones. As far as the latter are concerned, my policy is to request actors to leave them turned off at all times during rehearsals, since they can be incredibly irritating, and can easily disrupt a creative atmosphere.

A good stage manager will let the company know what they can and cannot do in the rehearsal room without sounding like some authoritarian school teacher. Actors are, on the whole, a very compliant group of people, and if approached in the right manner, are normally very obliging.

The read-through

Not every director will expect to do a read-through of the script on the first day of rehearsals, and often with shows which are through-sung or which contain a large amount of music, such as *Jesus Christ Superstar*, or *Hair*, there is little point in trying to tackle the piece in this way. However, with a musical which has a significant amount of script, such as *Guys and Dolls*, *My Fair Lady*, or *Fiddler on the Roof*, it is probably worth spending a couple of hours reading through the text so that collectively the actors can start to familiarise themselves with the piece. If the cast members have been sent scripts before the beginning of rehearsals, they may well have read through the material already, but often this will not be the case, and they will see the scripts for the first time at the read-through.

This read-through can often be a nerve-wracking occasion, both for the actors and the director, and for this reason it is most important to keep it as relaxed and informal as possible. The actors should not be encouraged to give a 'performance', since they will probably still be fairly unfamiliar with the material, and will inevitably be stabbing in the dark to some extent. It should be stressed that the read-through is really just a means of enabling everyone in the company to start to get to grips with the piece, to understand the story, and to begin to differentiate between the characters. Of course, whatever the director says, there will always be some actors who feel that they must give their all, and some who will go so far in the opposite direction that they will give an entirely colourless reading of their role. The fact is, in my opinion, it doesn't really matter; the read-through is always going to be a slightly uncomfortable process since it is usually the first time that the individual performers have had to act in front of one another. Once the reading is over, however, everyone will feel relieved, and a small mountain will have been scaled.

As I have said, not all directors will feel the necessity to have a read-through on the first day, and some musicals simply don't lend themselves to this approach anyway. Some directors will want to get straight down to the task of blocking the show, others will prefer to use improvisation as a means of experimenting with some basic ideas. There are many ways of beginning the rehearsal process, and no one method is necessarily better than another. Personally I prefer to avoid any specific staging on the first day, and I am also wary of improvisation at this early stage since it can seem very intimidating to a group of actors who are only just beginning to get to know each other. If I still have time after the read-through, I will often get the actors playing some very basic games. Alternatively, I will sometimes ask the choreographer to do a basic dance warm-up, followed by some more specific dance work relating to the choreographic style of the show. The musical director may also want to spend some time with the cast, checking their vocal ranges, and splitting them into their particular vocal groups (bass, tenor, mezzo soprano, etc.).

Theatre games

In these early stages of rehearsal, theatre games are often used to help the actors loosen up and lose their inhibitions, while also encouraging them to work together in a playful, unpressured atmosphere. Since most of us have a child lurking somewhere within, actors usually respond very well to these games and will throw themselves wholeheartedly into pursuits more often identified with the playground than the rehearsal room. Every director will have a different stock of games to draw from, and he or she will need to tailor them to suit the specific requirements of the group, whether it be a class of school children, a group of students or a cast of professional actors.

Of course there are hundreds of games that can be used to help break the ice in the rehearsal room, and many directors will adapt these, or make up new ones to suit their particular production. The following are just a few examples of theatre games which I have used in the past. Since they are fairly energetic, I have found them to be particularly useful with groups of students.

The naming game

This is a good way to kick off, especially if most of the cast are unknown to each other. A smallish, soft ball should be used for this game (the type supplied in juggling kits is particularly good).

1 The actors should be asked to stand in a circle: if the cast is a large one, it should be split into several circles so that each person is never too far away from the person opposite.

2 Before the ball is brought into play, each actor in turn should clearly call out his or her name.

3 The ball should then be passed to one of the actors, and that actor should then throw the ball to someone else in the group. As the ball is thrown, the person throwing should say the name of the person catching the ball. As the actor catches the ball, he or she should repeat their own name, then throw the ball to somebody else, calling out the receiver's name as they throw. In this way the ball is thrown about the circle in no particular order. This process should be repeated a number of times until everyone has had a reasonable chance to learn the names of all the players in the game.

A similar game can be used to test concentration; this time the 'naming' element can be used or disregarded at the director's discretion. The actors are asked to repeat the process just described, the only difference being that they are instructed to sit down on the floor once they have thrown the ball. The actors are then told that anyone sitting down can no longer receive the ball. Since this is the case, it follows that the ball will be passed to each member of the group only once before everyone is sitting on the floor. The group should be told before they start to memorise the sequence, i.e., to remember exactly who they throw the ball to. After they have completed this sequence once (see example overleaf), they should then be instructed to stand up and repeat the throwing pattern until told to stop. Once the sequence has been well established, a second ball can be introduced into the circle, following the same throwing pattern as the first. This may cause some momentary confusion, but the actors should soon get used to having to work with the two balls instead of just one. And finally, to test the concentration of the actors even further, a third ball can be introduced into the circle.

Once the actors have got the hang of this (and it is actually quite a lot simpler than it sounds!), the balls should be taken away and the same game played, but with the cast miming throwing and receiving the balls. This actually requires a greater degree of concentration than before, since there are no longer any tangible objects flying about the circle.

Fruit bowl

This very simple game, which is rather like musical chairs without the music, is a good way of getting the actors up on their feet and moving about.

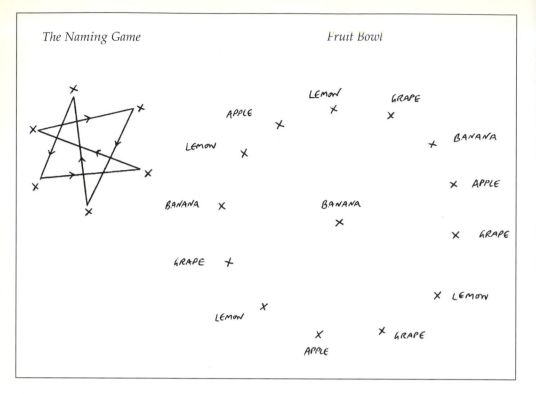

The Naming Game   Fruit Bowl

1   One actor should be placed in the middle of a circle of chairs. The chairs should be evenly spaced out, and the rest of the group should sit down, one on each chair. The person in the middle is the only player who does not have a chair to sit on.

2   Depending on the number of actors involved in the game, the players should be divided up into three or four different groups, each group having the name of a type of fruit. It is best to make sure that the individual members of each team are mixed up so that actors are not sitting beside other members of their own group (see example).

3   Once the actors are all seated, the actor in the middle calls out the name of one of the other groups. If the call is 'apples', for example, all the members of the apple group must change seats as quickly as possible, and the person in the centre must try to get a seat too. Usually this will mean that someone else ends up without a seat. However, if the person in the middle calls out 'fruit bowl', all the actors must change places with each other.

This game should be played as a warm-up exercise, and care should be taken to prevent it becoming too unruly. If actors start getting a little too boisterous, the director should find ways of penalising them; for example, insisting that the offenders must hop on one leg for the rest of the game.

The ring of glass

This is a game which I often use to calm things down, usually after the more frenetic activities such as those that I have just described. It is a variation on a game called the Glass Cobra, which Augusto Boal describes in his book *Games For Actors And Non-Actors*.

1 The actors, who are dispersed about the room, are asked to shut their eyes and keep absolutely silent. The director then gently leads each actor into a circle, ensuring that everyone is holding hands with the person on either side. They should now be instructed to find out, by touch alone, as much as they can about the hands which they are holding: whether they are large or small; whether the backs of the hands are hairy or smooth; and whether the nails are long or short or jagged. Several minutes should be enough for this purpose.

2 The director should then gently lead each actor out of the circle until everyone is once again dispersed about the room, preferably in different places this time. Eyes should remain shut, and no speaking or giggling should be allowed.

3 When the director gives the word, the actors should be asked to regroup in the circle, ensuring by touch alone that the people on the right and left are the same as before. This may take a considerable amount of time, and the actors should be told that once they are convinced that they have completed the task, they should wait patiently for further orders. When the director is finally satisfied that the ring of glass has been reassembled, the actors should be instructed to open their eyes again.

This exercise provides a very good contrast with the more energetic games previously mentioned, and it encourages the actors to focus on touch, one of the senses which is very often taken for granted.

The first day of rehearsals should be an opportunity for everyone to start to get to know the show, and to get to know each other. Some of the actors will already be well acquainted with the songs, having listened to previous cast recordings and perhaps seen filmed versions of the musical. Others may have little or no prior knowledge of the piece. By the end of the first day, however, everyone should at least have a taste of what the show is about, and what the style of this specific production is likely to be. As a director, I am very conscious of trying to create a company of actors who will work together to bring out the best in the show. By making the actors feel welcome on the first day of rehearsals, and by showing them that they are valued members of the company, a small step will have been taken towards turning this disparate group of performers into a team.

8 · Rehearsals – creating a company

From the very start of rehearsals, the actors should be encouraged to work together. In my experience, there is nothing so divisive as the principal/ensemble mentality, and the actors should try to think of the show as a group effort which relies on the commitment and enthusiasm of every single member of the team. Of course, some performers will have much larger roles than others; they will consequently feel a greater sense of responsibility and this will often create a greater sense of pressure too. Nonetheless, every member of the company has a contribution to make, and should approach the work with the same level of professionalism and commitment (and this goes for any production, whether it be professional or amateur). Where possible I try to avoid using the terms 'principals' and 'chorus', since it seems to me that everyone is really part of an *ensemble*; some actors just happen to have larger roles than others. 'Chorus' is a word I try to avoid altogether, since it implies a group of people all doing the same thing. 'Ensemble', on the other hand, suggests a collection of individuals, each with different identities and ideas.

Of course in reality an egalitarian approach isn't always appropriate. While this may work perfectly in a drama school, or a small repertory company, it is often the case with large commercial musicals that several 'star' names are needed to pull in the crowds, and celebrities often bring with them large egos, and defined ideas about company status. In these situations, the director will have to assess the situation accordingly, and try to find ways of integrating the celebrity into the cast. Fortunately most directors do not have to worry about celebrities and their egos, and this problem of integration is therefore not an issue.

Research

It is often a good idea during the first few days of rehearsal to encourage the actors to do some research on the piece. This can mean going back to the original source material for more detailed information about characterisation and historical detail, or it can involve making a more general investigation into the specific period in which the story is set, or exploring some other relevant piece of background information. For a recent production of *Kiss of the Spiderwoman*, for example, I asked the student cast to do some background reading about

64

Amnesty International and human rights abuses in South America. We then pooled the information and discussed our findings. The ensuing debate was both fascinating and horrifying, and helped to give everyone a much clearer idea about the disturbing issues with which this musical is concerned.

The research process is useful in several ways. Firstly, and most obviously, it helps to give the actors some very useful information about the piece which they are performing, and secondly it forces them to immerse themselves in the project from the start. Once they begin to feel that they have something to contribute to the discussion, they will usually start to get more involved with the piece. By getting the actors to do some of the research work, the director is actually making them an integral part of the whole process. In my experience, this is something to which most actors respond extremely well.

Group activities

There are, of course, other ways to help the performers familiarise themselves with the subject matter of the show. I was recently involved in a production of *Jesus Christ Superstar*, and we started rehearsals by watching edited highlights from various films concerning the life of Christ, such as Martin Scorsese's *The Last Temptation of Christ*, Pier Paolo Pasolini's *The Gospel According to St. Matthew*, and Denys Arcand's *Jesus of Montreal*. These three films, though vastly different in the treatment of their subject matter, all gave us valuable insights into the story of Christ's life, and provided lots of topics for discussion. This proved to be a very helpful way of kick-starting the whole project.

In a similarly biblical vein, several years ago I worked on a production of the Stephen Schwarz/John Caird musical *Children of Eden*, a show which focuses on two major parts of the Old Testament; the Creation and Noah's Flood. Most of the cast were required to play animals at some point in the show, and for research we were encouraged to visit London Zoo and observe in minute detail the physical behaviour of the animals. Back in the rehearsal room we talked about our discoveries, and did some lengthy improvisations based on our zoological observations. Again this research not only provided us with invaluable material (which later became an intrinsic part of the show), but also helped to unite the members of the company, and to create a real ensemble in which everyone played an important part.

Similar group projects could be devised for various other shows; for example, a company preparing a production of Cy Coleman's *Barnum* would be well advised to visit a circus to examine at first hand the mysteries of this unique form of entertainment. Likewise, a company in rehearsal for *Sunday in the Park with George* might draw inspiration from a group outing to an art gallery, where the actors could examine for themselves the 'colour and light' so often referred to in Stephen Sondheim's lyrics.

Improvisation

Whereas theatre games such as the ones described in chapter 7 tend to be fairly general, and do not, necessarily, rely on any particular acting ability on the part of the participants, improvisations are usually more specific, and more demanding. In my experience, these exercises tend to be more successful once the actors have had some opportunity to get to know each other, and for this reason, I usually get the cast to play a few theatre games before launching into the more taxing area of improvisation.

Some theatre directors have no patience with this type of exploratory work, and prefer to get straight down to the nuts and bolts of the text and the music. Others find it absolutely vital, and will happily spend days exploring the piece in this way. Of course, if the rehearsal time is limited, there will be a pressure to get the show on its feet as quickly as possible, and there may therefore be very little time for improvisatory work.

As a director, I have no hard and fast rules about improvisation – I use it in some circumstances and not in others. Students, I find, are often very receptive to this sort of work, whereas some experienced professionals find it indulgent and time-wasting. I believe that it can be an extremely useful method of enabling the actors to explore their characters, and in the best situations can also help to bring everyone in the company together.

The following few examples are exercises which I have sometimes used in the early stages of rehearsals: the first exercise is unrelated to the show being rehearsed, while the second and third begin to explore particular characters and situations from the musical itself.

News story

For this exercise the cast is split into fairly small groups of perhaps six to eight actors. Each group is given a different newspaper clipping which has a strong story-line, usually of no more than ten to fifteen lines, such as this one from the *Independent*, 28 July 1998.

> **Pilot Takes Passengers Hostage** A British pilot was questioned by Italian police after allegedly holding passengers 'hostage' on his aircraft when no one owned up to illegally smoking on board, it emerged yesterday. Captain David Hodgson, 57, was told someone had been smoking in a toilet on a Milan-bound flight of British Airways' low-cost airline, Go. He informed the Italian police and kept the 148 passengers in their seats for 40 minutes on landing in Italy. But police then boarded the flight and detained Captain Hodgson for allegedly holding the passengers against their will.

1 Once the groups have read their specific excerpt, they are then instructed to find a way of telling their story in a series of four tableaux. For example, they are told to imagine that a film has been made of this story, and that they are

allowed to present only the frozen frames of four key moments in the story. The actors are then given several minutes to organise this. They then present their frozen tableaux to the other groups, who are encouraged to guess what the story-line is. The watching groups should not be told whether they have guessed the story correctly or not.

2   The director should then instruct the groups to present another version of the story. This time they are allowed to mime the sequence of events, but the mime must not last longer than a specified amount of time, such as one minute. Again the groups are given a few minutes to organise this, and are then asked to present their mime to the other groups. The same procedure takes place as before, with the other groups guessing the story-line, or improving on their first interpretation of it. Again they are not to be told whether their guesses are correct or not.

3   Finally, the director asks each of the groups to present their story once more. This time the characters can speak, but they are only allowed one sentence per actor. Once again the groups are given several minutes to sort this out, and they are then instructed to present their story to the other groups. Finally the director can ask a member from each team to read out the original clipping, so that the other groups can find out how close they were to getting all the facts of the story.

The object of this exercise is fairly clear; by finding three different methods of presenting the same story, and therefore having to communicate specific information in three very different ways, the ingenuity of the group of actors is put to the test, and everyone is forced to start thinking as a team, as opposed to a group of individuals.

The train carriage

In this exercise, the director sets up a make-shift train carriage by placing two rows of chairs opposite each other, and indicates to the acting company where the door and the windows of the carriage are located. The director then goes round the company and gives each actor a number and a particular character trait, for example; intellectual, irritating, disruptive, aggressive, etc. The actors are then told that when the director taps them on the shoulder, they are to enter the train carriage as their character and interact with the people in the carriage. From time to time the director will shout, 'train stopping', and will instruct several of the actors to leave the train by calling out their numbers. While the actors are improvising in the carriage the director may feed in some other information, such as: 'the train stops in the middle of a tunnel, and the lights in the carriage suddenly go out.'

This exercise is obviously based on character, and gives the actor the opportunity to concentrate on fairly specific character details. Once the actors have experimented with this idea, the director may want to give them characters from the show to improvise with, and not necessarily the character that they themselves are actually going to play. The exercise is often useful in helping the actors to start creating characterisations for themselves, and it is particularly good for inexperienced actors since it is not too nerve-wracking, the train carriage being filled with other characters too.

Improvisation around specific scenes

Sometimes it can be very useful to take a scene, or a situation from the show, and improvise around it. For example, the first act of the Stephen Schwarz/Joseph Stein musical *The Baker's Wife* opens with a scene centred around a small village café in Provence, which slowly introduces the audience to various characters in the village. The café is clearly an important focus for the community and is the place where the villagers go to laugh, to gossip, and to argue.

A useful improvisation for this particular musical would be to set up a make-shift café in the rehearsal room, using tables, chairs, glasses, and bottles, and to nominate several actors as waiters and waitresses. The rest of the cast should be encouraged to invent characters from the village community; some may be in family groups of three and four, others may be solitary. At this stage it does not really matter who plays which character, and sometimes it is better to specify that actors who have been cast in specific roles in the musical should attempt a different character for this early improvisation. Once the café scene has been established, the director may want to add some colour by suggesting to one of the actors that he tries to pick someone's pocket, or that he suddenly finds something unexpected in his soup.

This sort of group improvisation can be very useful, especially for actors in the ensemble, since they can begin to work on a specific identity for their character, rather than simply trying to play a nebulous 'villager'. If an actor decides that he is the local postman; that he is in love with one of the waitresses in the café; that he has a personal vendetta against the village butcher and that he has a penchant for red wine, then the ensemble scenes in which he is involved will take on several new layers, and will consequently appear more detailed and textured to the audience.

Since this particular musical is so clearly concerned with the everyday lives of these Provençal villagers, character work in this show is going to be especially important. Consequently it is vital that the actors know exactly where they fit in to the community, and how they relate to the other people on stage. Improvisation can be a great help with this sort of detailed work.

Another example of a show where experimental character work can pay dividends is *West Side Story*, Bernstein's vibrant reworking of Shakespeare's *Romeo and Juliet*. Since the main focus for this musical is the rivalry between two opposing gangs, the Jets and the Sharks, it is vital that the distinct identity of each of these groups is clearly recognisable to the audience. In the first Broadway production of this piece, the actors playing Jets and those playing Sharks were actually kept apart during rehearsals, so that relationships developed in each separate group, but not between the two sets of actors. While this may seem like a rather extreme rehearsal technique, it is easy to see where the decision to segregate the two groups came from. Just as effective, in my opinion, would be some detailed character work and some separate group improvisation, focusing on developing the friendships, tensions, and jealousies which would naturally exist within two groups of headstrong teenagers.

Structuring rehearsals

Assuming that the production being mounted is a new one, there is no way that the director will be able to prepare a detailed rehearsal schedule for the whole period from day one of rehearsals, since there are far too many variables to take into account. Every group of actors has a different working dynamic, each production team will have different priorities, and every show will have different requirements. Because the theatre is, thankfully, mainly concerned with people, as opposed to machines, there is always going to be some uncertainty regarding how best to get from A to B, and how long it will take.

However, this need not mean that rehearsals descend into chaos. The director should try to have some sort of overview, and he or she should be aiming to achieve certain goals at specific key points in the schedule. The example of a skeleton rehearsal schedule shown overleaf is by no means the solution for every show and for every set of circumstances. However, it is a basic plan, setting achievable goals for the rehearsal of a two-act musical (lasting roughly two and a half hours) over a period of four weeks.

As I have already suggested, there never seems to be ample time to rehearse a musical, and although it would be perfectly easy to spend weeks rehearsing the first couple of scenes, it is important to be practical about what is achievable in the available time. The rough rehearsal schedule, although only a guideline, helps to prevent the director from being over-indulgent with some sections of the show, while neglecting others. In brief, this skeleton schedule is geared towards providing time for three full run-throughs in the final week of rehearsals, before moving to the theatre. Week one is largely spent learning the score, and starting work on choreography and ensemble staging. Week two concentrates on working through Act I, culminating in a stagger-through of the act at the end of the week. Week three follows the same pattern, this time for Act II, and the first half of week four involves detailed work on the whole show. For the three final run-throughs, the actors should be 'off the book' (i.e., without scripts), and the lighting designer should be in attendance for as much of the time as possible. For the very last run, rehearsal props should be replaced with show props, and costumes should be worn if they are available.

Once the rehearsal process has begun, the director will, of course, need to divide up each week into specific rehearsal blocks. Some directors draw up an entire plan for a whole week, while others, myself included, find it more practical to plan a day or two in advance. Since it is never really possible to envisage how long a scene or

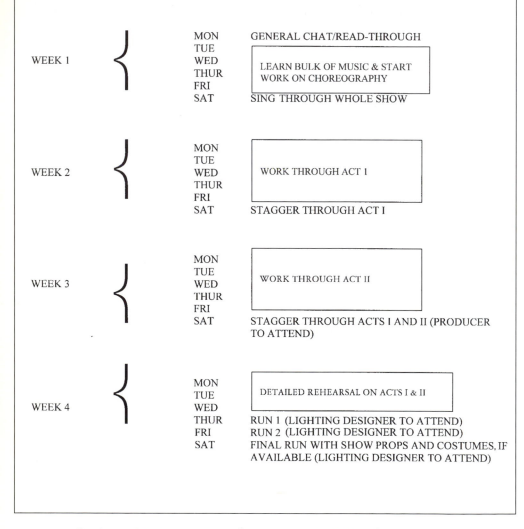

SKELETON REHEARSAL SCHEDULE

WEEK 1

MON	GENERAL CHAT/READ-THROUGH
TUE	
WED	LEARN BULK OF MUSIC & START WORK ON CHOREOGRAPHY
THUR	
FRI	
SAT	SING THROUGH WHOLE SHOW

WEEK 2

MON	
TUE	
WED	WORK THROUGH ACT 1
THUR	
FRI	
SAT	STAGGER THROUGH ACT I

WEEK 3

MON	
TUE	
WED	WORK THROUGH ACT II
THUR	
FRI	
SAT	STAGGER THROUGH ACTS I AND II (PRODUCER TO ATTEND)

WEEK 4

MON	DETAILED REHEARSAL ON ACTS I & II
TUE	
WED	
THUR	RUN 1 (LIGHTING DESIGNER TO ATTEND)
FRI	RUN 2 (LIGHTING DESIGNER TO ATTEND)
SAT	FINAL RUN WITH SHOW PROPS AND COSTUMES, IF AVAILABLE (LIGHTING DESIGNER TO ATTEND)

a song will take to block, I prefer to have more flexibility than a weekly schedule will allow. Nevertheless, I always try to keep the skeleton schedule at the back of my mind, so as not to lose sight of the overall picture.

9 · Rehearsals – songs, scenes, choreography and staging

Some of the best musicals are those which seem to flow seamlessly from scene into song, and from song into dance. In rehearsals, however, the different disciplines are very often divided up, ensuring that the actors are kept as busy as possible, and that every available moment is used to the full.

Split calls

Musicals are a unique form of theatre in that they always involve a combination of disciplines, usually acting, singing, and dancing. This means that there is a huge amount of work to cover. With a play there is usually only one set of rehearsals going on at any one time; this is not however an efficient way of organising rehearsals for a musical. So, if extra rehearsal space is available, it makes very good sense to split calls, so that the director can work with a group of actors in one room, while the musical director or the choreographer works with another group somewhere else. It is even possible to have a third set of rehearsals going on at the same time if the schedule will allow for it and if there are enough spare rehearsal rooms. The advantages are obvious; in this way the rehearsal time is used very efficiently, and the actors are kept as busy and stimulated as possible.

When drawing up a rehearsal schedule it is important to try, where possible, to be specific about the actors required for each call. Obviously it is not always possible to know how much will be achieved in any one rehearsal, and if an actor does not appear until the end of the scene, he or she may well have to wait around for a while, and sometimes may not be used at all. This is occasionally unavoidable, but it really is worth trying to make sure that it is the exception rather than the rule. There is nothing worse than a room full of disgruntled actors who have been sitting around for hours, having achieved nothing. A typical split call for a production of *Hot Mikado*, (adapted from the Gilbert and Sullivan opera by Rob Bowman and David H. Bell) is laid out overleaf.

When adopting this type of scheduling it is very important to make sure that the actors are never double-booked, and that while rehearsing one discipline they are not missing something relevant in another rehearsal. It is also important that rehearsals are not so carefully dove-tailed that the individual members of the production team are prevented from attending rehearsals other than their own. By this I mean that it is not healthy for the director, musical director, and choreographer to work in isolation all the time: the choreographer will almost

HOT MIKADO – REHEARSAL SCHEDULE

MONDAY 18TH MAY

	Main Hall (With Choreographer)	Music Room (With Director and M.D.)
10.00 – 12.00	Male Ensemble (Dance Recap) *Song: We Are Gentleman of Japan*	Yum-Yum / Nanki-Poo *Song: This Is What I'll Never Do*
12.00 – 1.00	Full Ensemble / Mikado *Song: The Mikado Song (Dance Break)*	Yum-Yum *Song: The Sun and I*
1.00 – 2.00	LUNCH	
2.00 – 4.00	Nanki-Poo / Male Ensemble *Song: A Wand'ring Minstrel, I*	Pish-Tush / Female Ensemble *Song: Braid The Raven Hair*
4.00 – 6.00	Full Company (Director & M.D. to join) *Song: Finale – Act II*	

certainly want some input from the director; the director will no doubt want to be present at some of the vocal calls; and the musical director will need to be very clear about the way that the choreographer is responding to the dance sections, especially if he or she is likely to be conducting the show in performance. So although having split calls can be a great benefit, it should not be forgotten that much of the important work will probably be collaborative and the director, musical director, and choreographer will need time to work together.

Music rehearsals

As I have indicated in the skeleton rehearsal schedule on p.70, it often makes sense to learn the bulk of the music in the first week. The reason for this is simple – it often takes a while for an actor to really assimilate the musical numbers, and if the score is a complicated one, such as Sondheim's *Sweeney Todd*, or Bernstein's *West Side Story*, it helps to learn the music early, and to keep brushing it up as rehearsals progress. If the actors are to be singing and dancing at the same time, it will make their lives much easier if they can get the music under their belts before having to tackle the choreography. Of course, as they are learning the steps they will probably forget some of the music temporarily, but if it has been well taught, and the actors have had time to absorb it properly, it will soon come flooding back.

While every musical director will have a different approach to rehearsing the music, most will want to start teaching the score as quickly as possible. Some will insist that the actors bring with them a tape-recorder, so that individual solos and harmony lines can be recorded and committed to memory later. In most cases the musical director is also an accomplished pianist and will often teach the score from the piano. Ideally there will also be a rehearsal accompanist who will be available to play whenever the musical director wants to concentrate solely on the singers. In my experience, many singer/actors are either unable, or very slow to read music, and most musical directors will have to bash out solo and harmony lines until they begin to stick. This is where tape-recorders can save a lot of time.

Once the actors have actually learned their specific vocal lines, they should be encouraged to memorise them as soon as possible, so that when it comes to staging the numbers, they will be 'off the book'. This makes life easier both for the director, who will find it most frustrating trying to stage sections of the show with the cast peering into their music, and for the actors themselves, who will be much freer to explore the possibilities of the scene if they are unencumbered by heavy musical scores.

Once the music has been learned, it is a good idea for the musical director to have occasional musical rehearsals, just to check that harmony lines are being remembered correctly, and that the actors are not being too free with their interpretation of the music. It is amazing how the musical phrasing, tempos, and dynamics of a score can alter as the actors become more confident with the material. In many cases this is a good thing, and many wonderful musical discoveries can be made during the rehearsal process. However, it is important that the musical director keeps a close eye on these developments, and that the actors are not allowed to feel that they can alter the music at will. A particular disease that often seems to spread through musical theatre casts is 'back-phrasing', a term which actually means singing behind the beat. It is often a result of over-indulgence on the part of the performer, and is an affectation which needs to be closely monitored by the musical director. Back-phrasing can, on the odd occasion, be an effective means of expression, but when used indiscriminately, it can be extremely irritating.

Warm-ups

Most musical directors will have their own approach to vocal warm-ups, and although they will usually be prepared to spend five or ten minutes going through some vocal exercises with the cast, many would maintain that it is not their responsibility to make sure that the actors are in a fit state, vocally, to start the rehearsal. As long as the rehearsal schedule states clearly what the purpose of each rehearsal will be, the actor should always ensure that he or she is ready for that rehearsal, and this goes for both singing and dancing too. If the musical director (or choreographer) then decides to do a warm-up before the rehearsal proper begins, this should be seen as an added bonus. Personally, I find that vocal warm-ups can be a very good way of beginning a rehearsal, not so much because of the effect they have on the individual voices, but more because of the effect that they have on the group as a whole. A good vocal warm-up not only helps to focus everyone's mind on the rehearsal ahead, but is an activity that everyone can do *together*, and therefore helps to remind the cast members that they are all part of the same team. Similar benefits can be gained from a good dance warm-up, or a few well-chosen theatre games.

Dance rehearsals

In an ideal situation the choreographer will be well prepared for rehearsals and will have discussed with the director in detail what the choreographic style of the show should be. He or she will also have discussed the allocation of work, deciding who is to take responsibility for which numbers in the show. Of course, with many musicals there are obvious dance sections, such as the dream ballet in *Oklahoma!*, and the high school prom in *Grease*. However, the line between what is danced, what is staged, and what is acted, is often somewhat blurred, and many directors may prefer to work in tandem with their choreographer on sections of the show which refuse to fall into any specific category. I will discuss such collaborative work later in this chapter, (see p.79), but for the time being I shall concentrate on the sections of the show that are purely danced, and which are therefore mainly the responsibility of the choreographer.

Rehearsal time is precious, and inspiration does not always strike when it is most required; for both these reasons it is a good idea for the choreographer to have a relatively clear idea of how to approach a dance section before the rehearsal begins. Sometimes he or she will have an assistant who will help in the planning stages, and more often than not a dance captain will be selected from amongst the performers, who may also act as an assistant, if required. Despite this back-up, choreographers who do no preparation may find themselves coming unstuck in the rehearsal room. With a basic structure, however, there is always something to fall back on, even if inspiration is lacking during the rehearsal.

Planning the dance sections

Many musical scores, especially the more old-fashioned ones, indicate specific sections of dance music, and very often the choreographer is expected to come up with something suitable to sustain these moments. However, the director should think very carefully about the reasons for having dancing at this point in the story, and should be very clear about what the dance is all about. Perhaps in the original production a section of dance was written in because of a specific performer's particular dance ability. This is not necessarily a good reason for keeping it in the show, and if it fails to provide any extra information about the story, or about certain characters' emotions, then it may just be redundant. (If a dance section is to be cut, it is important to check with the rights holding company before doing so). Dance for dance's sake is very seldom effective in a narrative musical, and the director and choreographer should try where possible to find a reason for the existence of these danced sections. The director's job should be to help give a context to any dancing in the show – it is not enough to expect the choreographer to come up with a succession of stunning dance steps to fill the gaps.

Once the choreographer and director have talked through the reasons for a particular choreographed section, the work can begin. As I mentioned earlier in the chapter, the rehearsal will usually begin with a dance warm-up, but the performers shouldn't think of this as a right; it is each individual's responsibility to prepare for rehearsals, and no-one should expect the choreographer to do that job for them. Often, however, the dance warm-up provides a good opportunity for the choreographer to work through specific steps which may later be incorporated into the show. Also, if the style of dance required for the piece is particularly distinctive, the choreographer may wish to work this in at the warm-up stage.

The dance warm-up may be accompanied by the rehearsal pianist (or *répétiteur*), but usually the choreographer will provide his or her own prerecorded material. As far as the rest of the rehearsal is concerned, producers with big budgets will normally provide an accompanist, but it is often the case that the choreographer will have to make do with a recording, usually laid down by the musical director once specific speeds have been established.

It is most important during these choreographic sessions that the director has the opportunity to see some of the work developing; after all, there is no point in the choreographer working flat out on a dance routine, only to discover once the work is done that the director doesn't like it and that it will need to be completely altered. As long as there is good communication between members of the production team, it should be possible to ensure that the separate departments are all working towards the same goal, and that stylistic unity is being preserved.

Rehearsing the scenes

As far as the staging of scenes is concerned, no two directors will work in exactly the same way. Some will come to the rehearsal with a very clear idea of staging, having already mentally 'blocked' the scene, while others will have no preconceived ideas and will wait until the actors are present before making any decisions about the staging. My method falls somewhere between the two. If the scene involves a handful of actors, I will certainly give the scene a lot of thought before entering the rehearsal room, but I try not to pre-block specific moves, since this can be extremely limiting for the performers. However, if the scene involves the ensemble, I will try to have a rough plan indicating where and when movement might take place. Having said this, I strongly believe that it is important to be flexible in the rehearsal room, and to work *with* the actors to achieve successful results. There is little point in casting a talented group of performers, and then simply imposing ideas upon them. Actors are not chess pieces, to be moved around the stage at the whim of the director; they are emotional and responsive, and if allowed to do so, will contribute enormously to the end result.

I usually begin the rehearsal with a read-through of the specific scene that is about to be staged. We will then discuss any questions or ideas that the scene throws up, and try to work out what motivates the characters. We will also look at how the scene relates to the rest of the show, and usually we will discuss what has happened immediately beforehand; i.e. what state of mind the characters are in when they enter the scene, and how they are affected by what they have just been doing. Depending on the group of actors that I have selected, and the time available, I will sometimes ask the performers to improvise the scene that has just taken place 'offstage', so that when it comes to rehearsing the scene in question, the actors have a very tangible idea of the events leading up to the current action. This process is exactly the same one that I use when directing a straight play; just because a piece involves dancing and singing does not mean that it should be treated with any less integrity.

This fairly serious approach is certainly suitable for musicals with well-written naturalistic dialogue, such as *Fiddler on the Roof*, but it will not always be appropriate for the more caricatured, stylised pieces such as *A Funny Thing Happened on the Way to the Forum*. For shows such as this one, which makes no pretence at naturalism, I would tend to concentrate on defining the characters, and finding a physical means of expressing each different role, rather than exploring general background and character history.

A Japanese Billy Bigelow discovers that his wife Julie is pregnant in *Carousel* (PHOTO: Toho Co. Ltd)

Having read through the scene, discussed it in some detail, and perhaps improvised around it, it is now time to put it on its feet. Some actors will try to be off the book for the very first staging rehearsals; others will steadfastly maintain that they cannot learn the script until they know exactly what they are doing in the scene (a fairly dubious claim, in my opinion). I am usually happy to let the actors use the script for the first staging rehearsal, but I try to impress upon them the need to get the lines under their belts for subsequent rehearsals. It is, after all, very difficult for the actor to be totally in character if he or she is still having to refer to the written text, and holding a script is clearly limiting in terms of physical movement. In my experience, a scene only really begins to take off once the lines have been learned and the actors are completely free and unencumbered.

Marking out the stage

On the practical side, before any staging work is undertaken, the stage management should ensure that the rehearsal room is 'marked out' correctly; i.e. that the specific dimensions of the set are clearly indicated on the rehearsal room floor with strips of coloured tape. All doorways and windows should also be indicated where possible, and if the set is designed as a series of levels, then this should also be shown on the 'mark-out'. If the set design incorporates furniture of any description, or a specific piece of set which the actors can use (a tree, a fence, or a lamp-post, for example), substitutes should be found until the proper set dressing is available so that the actors have something tangible to work with. Likewise, if it is decided that a specific character carries a stick, or wears glasses, or wields a gun, rehearsal props should be provided as soon as possible to represent these things. The sooner the actors get used to these 'personal props' the better.

Most directors will use some stage terminology to explain movement to the actors when rehearsing a scene. If an actor is asked to move 'upstage', he or she should move towards the back of the stage (or rehearsal space), and if requested to move 'downstage', should move towards the front. These expressions refer to the days when the floor of the stage was always angled up at the back and was therefore lower in front. 'Stage right' and 'stage left' are slightly confusing terms since, from the director's point of view, they are the opposite of what is expected. Assuming that the actor is facing out towards the imaginary audience, if requested to move 'stage right', it means that he or she should move to *his or her* right. Likewise, if asked to move 'stage left', the actor should move to the left, again assuming that he or she is facing the audience. These terms take a while to get used to, but are universally recognised in the theatre and should therefore be observed.

Achieving a creative atmosphere

First rehearsals are often a nerve-wracking experience for all concerned, and I believe that the director should try to make things as painless as possible for the actors. I try to ensure, during the early stages, that there are no unnecessary onlookers in the room, and that includes other members of the cast who may have wandered in from another rehearsal. The less the actors feel that they are on show the more relaxed they will feel, and the more productive the rehearsals will be. As the individual members of the company become increasingly familiar with each other, they will begin to be less self-conscious, and at this stage I will usually allow other cast members into the rehearsal room. The important thing is to let the actors feel that they can make mistakes during rehearsals without making fools of themselves, so if I feel that a comfortable, creative atmosphere is being jeopardised in any way, I will once again close the rehearsal room door.

Other factors can also affect the creative atmosphere in a rehearsal room. Obviously any intrusive noise from outside will weaken the concentration of the actors, and bad ventilation and inadequate heating can be very detrimental to the overall mood of the company. Just as important, though, is the attitude of those in the rehearsal room, and that includes all the stage management, the rehearsal pianists, and the other members of the production team. There is nothing worse, in my opinion, than somebody who is present in the room but shows no interest in the work in progress. A rehearsal accompanist, for example, who sits and reads the paper until he or she is required to play is really contributing very little to the whole process. Likewise, members of stage management who stand in the corner and chat while the director, musical director, or choreographer is busy trying to focus the energies of the cast, can be disruptive in the extreme. My attitude is that anyone who is present in the room should in some way contribute to the rehearsal in progress. If they are not able to do this, then they should not be in the rehearsal room.

Since the staging of a scene is so closely affected by the decisions of the director, and of the actors taking part, there is little point in this chapter in trying to dissect a specific scene from any particular show. Without the actors, directions to move stage right or stage left and so on are really meaningless. However, there are one or two points which may help to illustrate how to improve the quality of the work in the rehearsal room.

Individual involvement It is most important to make sure that everybody feels involved in the scene that is being rehearsed. This is not normally a problem with scenes featuring only a handful of actors, since each character will usually have some lines to speak, and some sort of attitude towards the scene that is taking place. With a large number of actors on stage, however, especially in scenes involving the entire ensemble, it is all too easy to fall into the trap of generalised reaction. In these larger ensemble scenes it is vital, in my opinion, to make sure that everyone knows who they are as characters, that they question the events taking place, and that they have an attitude towards them.

Just as a crowd of people waiting on a station platform will be made up of individuals with different backgrounds, different prejudices, and different sensibilities, so too should an ensemble on stage feel like a collection of individual personalities. This is the only way that naturalistic ensemble scenes will really take on a life of their own and feel spontaneous and convincing. (Of course, there are musicals where this approach would not necessarily be the correct one, such as highly stylised works like *The Rocky Horror Show*, or *Chicago* – but they tend to be the exception, rather than the rule.) Not only will the show benefit from such character detail, but the actors, particularly those playing small roles in the ensemble, will feel that they have a much more important contribution to make to the production as a whole.

Freedom of movement Trying to set moves early on in the rehearsal process before any experimentation has taken place is not usually a good idea.

Ultimately, of course, the cast will have to commit to certain staging decisions, and although there may be a fair amount of freedom within this, a pattern will need to be established. But to force the actors to commit to specific moves from early on in the rehearsal process is often counter-productive, since it is only once the actors have really begun to get to grips with their characters that they can start to feel comfortable with their moves. Often staging which seemed fine in the first few days of rehearsal will need to be adapted once the actors have really found their feet.

The term used to describe the actual position of the actors on stage and the moves which take place during a scene or song is blocking. Whatever process the director uses to stage the show, there will come a time in rehearsals when the moves of the actors need to be recorded by the DSM in the prompt book (see pp.94-5). This blocking will inevitably change to some extent once the production moves from the rehearsal room to the theatre, and once the director sees the actors on stage he or she will probably find better solutions to some of the staging problems. None the less, the blocking recorded in the prompt book is a very useful record, both for the director and stage manager, and also for the lighting designer when it comes to devising a lighting plot. The actors should also be encouraged to take responsibility for keeping notes about their own personal blocking. They usually do this by writing the specific moves in pencil in their scripts. When confusion arises, which it often does, the actor can always refer to the DSM and to the blocking details recorded in the prompt book.

Musical staging

Musical staging is a slightly ambiguous term which can cover anything from the simple blocking of a solo song, to the organisation of a huge ensemble number involving the whole cast. There are no hard and fast rules dictating who will take responsibility for the musical staging; in some cases it will be the choreographer, in others it will be the director, and often it will be a collaborative process involving the two of them. In effect, any section of the show which is neither a full dance routine, nor a passage of spoken dialogue, could be described as being suitable for musical staging. If there is movement and music involved, whether this music be vocal or purely instrumental, then some degree of musical staging may be required.

A good example of this is the 'Ascot Gavotte' from Lerner and Loewe's *My Fair Lady*. In the show, an ensemble of stiff-upper-lipped aristocrats sings this formal number to introduce the Ascot racing scene. It is intended to be highly stylised and to satirise the exaggerated characters who sing it. While it is clearly not a dance number, it will certainly require some suitable movement to mirror the stilted, cut-glass precision of the song. At the other end of the spectrum is a number such as 'A Wonderful Guy', sung by Nellie Forbush in Rodgers and Hammerstein's *South Pacific*. This is a joyous, vibrant number in which Nellie

Strangers on a train; a scene from the musical review *Closer Than Ever*
(PHOTO: Ashley Straw)

sings of her newly-discovered love for the French plantation owner, Emile de Becque. While this number has to have an energy and spontaneity about it, and should therefore not feel choreographed, it will undoubtedly benefit from some input from either the choreographer or the director to help give it shape. Spontaneity is actually rather difficult to portray on stage, and the actress playing the part will probably need some assistance in finding different ways to express Nellie's sense of exhilaration.

As I have already mentioned with reference to choreography, musical staging needs to be given a fair amount of thought before the rehearsal. It is certainly not advisable to set every move beforehand, thereby excluding the actors from any creative input, but it is important to have a basic framework for the number which can be developed once the actors start to work on the material. As a director, I find that collaboration with the choreographer can result in some very exciting discoveries. On a recent student production of *Hot Mikado*, for example, the choreographer and I tried to find time to experiment with staging ideas prior to rehearsals, so that when it came to working with the actors, we had plenty of different options to play with. For one number entitled 'And the Drums Will Crash', we decided that the stage should be bare except for the five actors involved in the song and a pile of suitcases. We then set about being as creative as possible with these limited resources, and very soon the suitcases had turned into an assortment of different things; an armchair, a staircase, the interior of a church, and a set of musical instruments. This really was a collaborative process, some discoveries being made by myself and the choreographer before rehearsals began, and some coming out of the work in the rehearsal room.

In my experience, the larger the number of actors on stage, the more important it is to do some planning prior to the rehearsal. This is partly because a large group of performers will very quickly lose patience if they are shut in a rehearsal room and made to wait around. But more importantly, whereas with a small group of actors it is possible for everyone to make some contribution, with a large ensemble it is simply not practical to allow everyone to have their say. In these circumstances, a democratic approach is most likely to descend into chaos.

Musical staging is essentially the art of bringing to life a section of the show which is sung or musically underscored. It is more complicated than it looks and requires some conscientious preparation, and some detailed work in the rehearsal room. Although I can provide no perfect guide to musical staging (since every production has different needs, and every actor will respond in a different way to the process) there are certain points which are well worth bearing in mind.

A patriotic scene from *Jack the Ripper* (PHOTO: Nick Davey)

Focus

It is most important to decide what the focal point of any scene should be. Many things will draw the eye of the audience, such as bright colours, or sudden movement, and the director or choreographer should try to ensure that the audience is drawn towards what it is intended to see. For example, in Lionel Bart's *Oliver!*, Nancy, with a little help from the ensemble, sings 'Oom-Pah-Pah!', a bawdy drinking song. This song is usually staged with great gusto, and lots of beer-drinking, tankard-clashing, and skirt-swishing. In short, the song is a good example of a number which requires staging, as opposed to choreography. But if there is too much 'business' going on behind Nancy, and the eye of the audience is drawn away from her, the lyrics and consequently the content of the song will be lost. This is a crude example, but it serves as a broad reminder that it is the job of the director or choreographer to make sure that any background activity supports the soloist, and helps to make sense of the story being told.

The actors on stage can also be very instrumental in helping to focus the attention of the audience. In *Jesus Christ Superstar*, for example, the character of Jesus enters the temple and finds that it is swarming with prostitutes, money lenders, and thieves. His sudden outburst, 'My temple should be a house of prayer', should silence the whole crowd and force everyone to notice him. However, if half the ensemble continue their activities, or even a handful of actors fail to pay attention to Jesus at this point, the focus of the scene will be split, and the dramatic effect will be weakened. The audience will always be interested in watching what the characters on stage are looking at, so the director needs to be quite decisive about the focus for any given scene. Sometimes the lighting will help to give emphasis to one particular character, or to one specific area of the stage, and in these situations other activities may continue in the background. However, as soon as the director begins to feel that the focus of the audience is in danger of being pulled in different directions, he or she must quickly try to address the problem.

Positioning the actors An actor will inevitably pull focus if he or she is in a commanding position on the stage. Height will always give an advantage, and an actor standing on a chair, a ladder, or a platform, will be in a particularly authoritative position. The centre of the stage is also a good place to command attention, not least because it is usually visible from every part of the auditorium. Whoever is responsible for musical staging may well decide to place an actor in one of these strong positions in order to emphasise something that he or she is singing, or even to help give stature to an actor who has little natural stage presence.

While on this subject, it is a good idea for the director or choreographer to try to use different levels and interesting areas of the stage to vary the picture and to keep the audience visually stimulated. I tend to think of the set as a big adventure playground, and consequently I am always keen to try out as many different staging ideas as possible. For example, if the set includes lamp-posts, pillars, or poles, I will always try to use them in the staging.

'I've Got a Little List' from *Hot Mikado* (PHOTO: Nick Davey)

Upstaging A common complaint from actors is that they are being 'upstaged' by other performers. This means that either there is distracting business occurring elsewhere during moments when the audience's attention should be fully upon the actor in question, or that in order to address one of the other characters, the actor is being forced to turn upstage, and therefore away from the audience. The former problem of pulling focus is a recurring one, and needs to be constantly monitored. Obviously actors' performances will change and develop during the run of a show, especially if the run is a long one, and they are often unaware that something that they have discovered in performance is actually very distracting to the audience. For this reason it is important that the director checks the show on a regular basis, or that a deputy is appointed to do so. The latter problem of positioning is easily rectified by ensuring that the actors who are listening are placed downstage of the actor who is singing, so that he or she can project out towards the audience as much as possible.

Although actors often become preoccupied by the problem of being upstaged, audiences are becoming increasingly accustomed to the fact that they may not be able to see the faces of the actors at all times. In theatres where the audience is seated on three sides of the stage, or indeed where the seating is in-the-round, with the audience completely surrounding the stage, it is accepted that the performers' faces will not be in view to everyone at all times, even when they are speaking or singing important material. Once this is taken on board by the audience, it is really not such a problem, as long as the voices of the actors can be heard at all times.

Coping with a large space Focus is often difficult to achieve in a large theatre where members of the audience are some distance from the actors. If there are lots of characters on stage, and the vocal line jumps from performer to performer as is the case with 'There is Nothing Like a Dame' from Rodgers and Hammerstein's *South Pacific*, it is often very difficult for the audience to make out who is actually singing, especially if the voices are artificially enhanced and therefore coming from speakers rather than directly from the actors themselves. In such cases, the director or choreographer needs to help the audience by shifting the focus clearly and deliberately. This can be done by asking an actor to leap onto a crate just before singing a solo line, for example; not only will the sudden movement grab the attention of the audience, but the actor will also be in a more commanding position to deliver the line.

Lyrics

It goes without saying that song lyrics are written to be heard, and are vital in terms of story-telling and character delineation. In opera, where lyrics are usually in a foreign language (or might just as well be), emotions often come across as more generalised and exaggerated, precisely because of this lack of clarity where lyrics are concerned. Personally I find this very frustrating indeed, and I therefore strive when working on a musical to make sure that the audience can hear every single word.

Firstly, it is important to keep reminding the actors in rehearsal about their diction, and to pull them up whenever the lyrics become muddy and indistinct. In accoustic productions, where there is no vocal amplification, it makes sense to try where possible to keep the actors facing the front if they are singing solo lines. Not only does this help with audibility, but also the audience is able to see the actors' faces and expressions, and therefore has a clearer idea about the meaning of the song. With an amplified show, especially one which uses float mikes or floor mikes, the actors will need to be aware of the microphone positions, so that they can direct their voices accordingly. Body mikes (i.e., radio microphones which are attached to the body of the actor), give the greatest degree of freedom, and will allow the actor to face away from the audience without any loss of vocal power. This is wonderfully liberating for the performer, but it should be remembered that depriving the audience of the sight of an actor's face for any length of time can be very counter-productive, since facial expression is such a clear indicator of a character's emotional state.

Who is the song directed at? On the subject of lyrics, it is also important to decide who is actually being addressed by the singer. This may seem a fairly obvious statement, but it is surprising how often this aspect of staging is overlooked. It is, of course, theatrical convention for a character alone on stage to voice his or her inner thoughts in the form of a song. A good example of this is 'Ice Cream' from Bock and Harnick's *She Loves Me*. In this song Amalia, a shop-girl, muses over a letter that she is writing to a blind date, while also fixating on the behaviour of George, one of her collegues from work. It is a wonderfully comic number which very successfully allows the audience to share in the anxieties, preoccupations, and excitements of this likeable young heroine. The song is clearly an internal monologue, and not intended to be 'heard' by anyone; only the audience is privy to Amalia's inner thoughts.

When staging this kind of song, there are two choices as far as focus is concerned; the character can either address the audience directly as though the inner debate has become externalised, or the audience can remain as onlookers, with the character expressing her inner thoughts, but not bringing the audience into the debate. Both these decisions are valid, but it is up to the director to decide which interpretation is best suited to the style of the production. It is then most important to be consistent with other similar moments in the musical. After all, it will be very confusing for the audience if this focus shifts constantly throughout the entire show.

Visual variation

In most cases the director will be particularly keen to vary the look of the stage picture so that the show remains visually as well as vocally stimulating. When moving the actors around the set, it is important to make sure that there is always some purpose for movement. An actor who suddenly wanders stage left for no apparent reason will almost certainly look unconvincing; but if there is some clear motivation, and he or she goes to look out of a window, or goes to talk to someone in a different area of the stage, then the move is much more likely to appear natural and unforced.

When attempting to manoeuvre a large crowd of actors across the stage it is usually best to try to split them into groups and to stagger the move. In real life it is very seldom that a group of people will suddenly decide to move *en masse*, and on stage this sort of collective decision will often look forced and unconvincing. When dealing with large groups, it is also best to avoid having the actors standing in lines, unless, of course, the scene has a particular formality that needs to be emphasised by the staging.

Treating the lyrics as text

With numbers involving only a few actors it is often a good idea, in the early stages of rehearsal, to separate the music and the lyrics and to encourage the performers to try acting through the song using only the latter. This takes away any vocal preoccupations which the singers might have, and allows them to concentrate exclusively on what is being expressed. In this way the song can be treated more like a scene, and the actors can experiment with different ideas without having to worry about timing or tuning. Once the actors have a really clear idea about exactly what is going on in the scene, the music can be reintroduced and some specific staging ideas can be developed.

Making use of instrumental sections In most cases, a song will have an instrumental introduction and passages of linking music between the choruses and verses. Some careful thought must go into the planning of these musical moments, since it is clearly not acceptable for the scene simply to grind to a halt before the next passage of singing occurs. Often these sections of music can be used to underscore a move into a new position, or perhaps, during the introduction, a lighting change will help to establish a new mood for the song.

Some numbers also have an extended musical section in the middle; 'I Don't Know How To Love Him' from *Jesus Christ Superstar* is a good example. The song is a personal outpouring from Mary Magdalene, who is

'Back on Base', a sultry jazz number from *Closer Than Ever* (PHOTO: Ashley Straw)

trying to make sense of the conflicting emotions which she has begun to feel for Jesus. Yet right in the heart of the number comes a passage of instrumental music. There is a danger here that the emotional force of the song will be dissipated by this musical interlude. It is up to the director, however, to use this music dramatically so that some action of Mary's at this point sustains the highly charged atmosphere that has already been created. Maybe she goes to kiss Jesus as he sleeps, or perhaps she momentarily decides to run away. The point is that sections of instrumental music such as this must always be seen in the context of the whole number; they should be used to sustain or heighten the emotions which are being expressed by the song, and should never simply feel like a self-indulgent moment of musical beauty.

Staging with props Sometimes the staging of a song can be aided by the use of props (as in the case of *Hot Mikado*, mentioned earlier in this chapter) or bits of

'What am I Doin'?' from *Closer Than Ever* (PHOTO: Ashley Straw)

costume. Actors often enjoy working out stage business with walking sticks, hats, and handkerchieves, etc., and the clever incorporation of such things into musical numbers can often be extremely effective. In a recent production of Maltby and Shire's *Closer Than Ever* which I directed, the character singing 'What am I Doin'?' made fantastic use of a silk scarf which had clearly been stolen from a girl who was fast becoming the object of his unhealthy obsession (see photograph). Likewise, in a production of *Oklahoma!* which I worked on several years ago, as Curly started to sing 'The Surrey with the Fringe on Top', he began to make an improvised carriage out of a box, two paraffin lamps, and some washing which was hanging down from a line. There was a naivety and innocence about this spontaneous behaviour which somehow fitted the mood of the song perfectly, and which contributed enormously to the overall effect of the scene.

Musical staging is, as I have suggested, something which takes a certain amount of skill and experience. Some directors will expect this work to be the responsibility of the choreographer, others will work in collaboration, and a few will undertake this aspect of staging themselves. Regardless of who actually takes on this responsibility, it is most important to ensure that the actors themselves make a note of any staging decisions which affect them. There is nothing more frustrating than experimenting with ideas in the rehearsal room, finally committing to a particular version of the staging, and subsequently discovering that the actors have forgotten the moves. The stage manager will, of course, try to keep a note of all blocking in rehearsals, but with complicated musical staging it is unrealistic to expect precise information about the movements of every single actor.

Specialists in the rehearsal room

Sometimes a director will decide to call in a specialist to help with some aspect of the show which lies outside his or her own particular field of expertise.

Accents

Many musicals require the actors to adopt a specific accent, and in order to give the show as authentic a sound as possible, it is often worth calling in the services of an accent or dialect coach. In situations where the budget is very tight, it may be worth asking around to see if anyone has a friend from the particular area in which the show is set. This may not be as effective as using an accent coach, since the native speaker may not be good at teaching others how to speak with an accent, but it is certainly better than nothing.

A large proportion of musicals are set in America, and although most actors will probably be able to have a stab at a generalised North American accent, many musicals require a more specific sound. For example, the setting for *Carousel* is the New England coast of Maine, and for *Oklahoma!* it is the mid-West. An accent coach will be able to give the cast some details about the particular accent or dialect, will often supply written notes on pronunciation, and will usually provide a voice tape with extracts read by native speakers. Other shows which would benefit from some help in this department are: *Cabaret* (many members of the cast are required to speak with a German accent); *Fiddler on the Roof* (most of the characters are Russian Jews); and *Once On This Island* by Ahrens and Flaherty (a rich, Caribbean fairytale).

Fights and physical skills

Specialists are often called in to help with the more physical aspects of a production. If the show requires fighting of any sort, or a specific display of swordsmanship, a fight director can be invaluable. Not only will a good fight director ensure that the stage action looks convincing, he or she will also show the actors the safest possible way of achieving the desired effect, whether it be a fight with knives as in the final scene of *Oklahoma!*, or a street fight between two rival gangs as in *West Side Story*. A show like Cy Coleman's *Barnum* will require specialist physical skills of a different sort, and any director undertaking this particular musical would be well advised to call in the help of a trained circus performer. A similar example is Kander and Ebb's *The Rink* which is, as the title suggests, set in a roller-skating rink, and requires some of the performers to skate. It is important, therefore, to make sure that they receive some expert advice on this.

Special tricks

Some shows will require illusions or magic tricks, and since this is an area which is foreign territory for most directors, it is usually the case that a consultant will need to be brought in. Shows which may require some assistance in this area are Ken Hill's *The Phantom of the Opera*, *Jack the Ripper*, by Pember and de Marne, and Arlen and Harburg's *The Wizard of Oz*.

Background information

On a less practical level, specialists may also be called in to help the cast get to grips with the subject matter of the show. For a recent production of *Jesus Christ Superstar*, for example, we brought in a vicar to provide some detailed background information about the life of Christ and the political situation in first-century Israel. Similarly, a cast of *Fiddler on the Roof* might greatly benefit from talking to a rabbi, or to some other member of the Orthodox Jewish faith. In short, any information which will help to provide the cast with a clearer idea of the specific world of the musical being rehearsed can only be to the advantage of all concerned.

Of course many producers will simply not have the finances to pay for expensive dialect coaches, fight directors and so on. In such cases it is well worth spreading the word, and asking the cast whether they have any friends or acquaintances with the necessary specialist skills. In the past I have often approached local drama schools to find out whether they have any information concerning a particular specialist. There is also a chapter in the theatrical publication *Contacts* (see appendix for details) which lists a whole range of different consultants.

In this chapter I have examined rehearsals with special reference to the creative team and the performers. In the following chapter I will go on to discuss the contribution of the stage management to the smooth running of this whole process. By dividing the subject of rehearsals into two parts, the one creative and the other practical, I do not mean to imply that they are somehow separate and unconnected. This is clearly not the case, but for the sake of clarity I have decided to treat them individually. In my view, a successful rehearsal period is one in which both the practical and the creative work together 'cheek by jowl'.

10 · Rehearsals –
stage management
responsibilities

The stage management team is responsible for running the rehearsal room, and for ensuring that the daily rehearsals run as smoothly and efficiently as possible (see Chapter 3 for a list of stage management duties). Before rehearsals begin it will be the stage manager's job to make absolutely certain that every member of the company receives a phone call and is given precise details concerning the venue for the rehearsals and the date and time when he or she is expected to attend for the first company meeting. If the director has any intention of getting the actors to do any physical activities on the first day, such as playing theatre games, or participating in a dance class, they should be prewarned by the stage manager so that appropriate clothing can be worn.

To ensure that the first day runs as smoothly as possible, the stage manager should check several important details:

- There should be enough chairs in the rehearsal room for the whole company, including the actors, the creative team and the stage management.

- Assuming that the director intends to have a read-through, there should be enough copies of the script for all the actors and the production team.

- There should be adequate supplies of tea and coffee so that refreshments are available throughout the day. This is particularly important on the first day, since the actors will need to get to know each other quickly, and taking breaks together is one way of achieving this.

(Some other stage management duties which apply particularly to the first day of rehearsals are mentioned in Chapter 7.)

The mark-out

The stage manager will need to discuss the mark-out with the director before the first day of rehearsals. If it looks likely that some staging work will be done at this early point, it is vital that the stage manager knows this so that he or she can arrange to get into the rehearsal venue beforehand, and do a thorough mark-out of the set. Before doing this, however, it is best to check certain details with the director. Often rehearsal rooms will have a mirror running the length of one wall, and some directors, expecially on shows which involve complex choreography, will want the actors to face this mirror so that dance steps can constantly be checked. The stage manager will therefore have to ensure that the mark-out takes this into account. There is nothing more frustrating for a stage manager than the discovery that the mark-out is the wrong way round and that the whole thing will have to be changed. It is also worth noting the position of the rehearsal room door. It can be very distracting for the actors if this door is clearly in view, and they can see people wandering in and out while they are trying to concentrate on performing. The stage manager should try, when doing the mark-out, to arrange things so that the door is upstage of the performing area.

It is also important to remember that the director will need to have some space in front of the stage area so that he or she can get an idea of how the show will look from the auditorium. If the director is pinned against the rehearsal room wall with the actors 'strutting and fretting' immediately in front, he or she will find it very hard to judge the work objectively. Also, later in the rehearsal process, it is useful for the stage manager to set up a production desk in front of the stage area so that the creative team can watch the show and take notes. There will need to be sufficient space downstage of the playing area to accommodate this.

Rolls of coloured tape are normally used for the mark-out, each colour representing a different element of the set. If the set is designed on various levels, the stage management may attempt to represent this by using suitably sized rostra. Once the mark-out has been completed, the stage manager should gather the company together and explain in detail how this two-dimensional representation relates to the set design. The actors should be encouraged to ask questions at this stage, since it is most important that they should be clear about the stage area and its advantages and limitations.

Schedules

During the first few days of rehearsals the director, together with the choreographer and musical director, will work out the first of a series of rehearsal schedules, usually planning one or two days in advance (although some directors will plan the whole week ahead). Often the stage manager will help with the planning of this schedule, and once it has been finalised, he or she will type it up and post it on the noticeboard. Alternatively, if the cast is a fairly small one, individual copies of the schedule may be handed round to each actor. The stage manager should take great care to ensure that the schedule is neatly laid out and unambiguous so that no confusions arise. There is nothing worse for a director than a half-attended rehearsal, so instructions to the actors need to be clear and precise (see the example overleaf from rehearsals for *Closer Than Ever*). The schedule should always include the following pieces of information:

- The date of the rehearsals.

- The venue for the rehearsals.

- The start time and the finish time of each rehearsal.

- The scenes which will be covered in each rehearsal (this is particularly important since the actors may need to familiarise themselves with the scene before attending the call).

- The names of the actors required for each rehearsal.

CLOSER THAN EVER

REHEARSAL CALL – THURS 9TH JULY '98

VENUE – PLEASANCE THEATRE REHEARSAL ROOM

11.00 – 13.00	ACT II -	"FANDANGO"	BEVERLEY KLEIN GARETH SNOOK
13.00 – 14.00	LUNCH		
14.00 – 15.15	ACT II -	"THE MARCH OF TIME"	HELEN HOBSON BEVERLEY KLEIN MARK McKERRACHER GARETH SNOOK
15.30 – 17.00	RUN ACT II		HELEN HOBSON BEVERLEY KLEIN MARK McKERRACHER GARETH SNOOK
17.15 – 18.00	WORK THROUGH NOTES		HELEN HOBSON BEVERLEY KLEIN MARK McKERRACHER GARETH SNOOK

THANK YOU

C. R. GEORGE.
STAGE MANAGER

Since it is the stage manager's responsibility to make sure that every actor knows when he or she is called for rehearsals, sometimes it will be necessary to telephone the actors at home. For this reason the stage manager must ensure that all contact numbers for the cast are up-to-date. As a safety net it is also sensible to give out a home phone number which the cast can ring if they have not been notified about the schedule for the following day. It makes sense if this number is the stage manager's; he or she simply needs to record the rehearsal call on the answerphone, and this will save anyone having to man the phone for hours on end.

The prompt book

The stage manager's prompt book is essentially the production bible – it contains all the information which is slowly gathered throughout the rehearsal period. By the time the show is ready to move into the theatre it is usually bursting with lighting cues, sound cues, and props lists, not to mention all sorts of other facts and figures relevant to the production.

Ideally the deputy stage manager will organise the prompt book prior to the first day of rehearsals. Then, as information is accumulated, such as contact numbers and lists of sound and lighting cues, they will immediately be filed in the book. It is usually constructed by taking the script and the score, dividing them into separate pages, and inserting them into a suitably sized ring-binder.

As in the example from *Into the Woods* (see pp.94-5), the left-hand page is divided into columns, where any important information concerning cueing, blocking, and prop-setting is noted down, and the right-hand page is the printed script or score. Although the example here is printed in black and white, the DSM will colour-code these instructions once he or she is satisfied that they are set in stone: a blue pen is usually used for any information concerning calls for actors; a red pen for any cue standbys (the warning that the DSM gives to the relevant department prior to the cue); and a green one for the actual cues. Any notes concerning blocking and prop-setting are usually made in pencil.

Once the production reaches the theatre, the prompt book becomes the nerve-centre for the whole show. For this reason it is vital that the DSM makes the notation clear and legible, so that if ever someone else is called in to cue the show at the last minute, they will be able to interpret the information correctly. The golden rule concerning the prompt book is that once it reaches the theatre, it must never be taken away. The reasons for this are obvious; if the book were to be mislaid, the show would probably have to be cancelled.

Prompting

During rehearsals, one of the stage managers (usually the DSM) should be 'on the book' at all times. This means that he or she should sit watching rehearsals, noting staging moves, adding new props to the props list, and ensuring that the actors

① S, S.M., L, F, enter through auditorium R doors, and up onto S.L. L + F have blind sticks. S has staff. S.M. has umbrella.

② W enters D.S.R.

③ B.W. moves away U.S.L.

④ B.W. moves back S.R.

⑤ SISTERS move further on stage (S.L.)

S/B LX Q 130

LXQ 130   GO ——

STANDBY

LXQ 131
SQ's 10 + 11

(STEWARD with wicker satchel and staff, STEPMOTHER with umbrella, CINDERELLA'S FATHER with carpet bag, LUCINDA and FLORINDA with blind canes and dark glasses. Bedraggled, THEY make their way downstage)

<u>BAKER</u>

The Steward and the royal family.

(THEY bow)

What brings you into the woods?

<u>STEPMOTHER</u>

The castle has been set upon by a giant.

<u>BAKER'S WIFE</u>

Oh, no….

<u>BAKER</u>

(To STEWARD)

I warned you! Why didn't you do something?

<u>STEWARD</u>

I don't make policy, I just carry it out!

(WITCH appears)

<u>WITCH</u>

(To BAKER)

And I warned <u>you</u> that you can't count on a royal family to solve your problems.

<u>BAKER'S WIFE</u>

I think it best we go back to the village.

<u>WITCH</u>

(Bitter)

I wouldn't be in such a rush if I were you. Guess which path the giant took to the castle?

<u>BAKER'S WIFE</u>

Oh, no…..

The prompt book: *Into the Woods* (courtesy of Josef Weinberger) stick to the script and do not start paraphrasing their lines. Prompting is a delicate job, and needs to be approached very sensitively. Once the actors are suitably comfortable about their lines, they will usually try to do without their scripts. At this point the stage manager will need to be on the alert, firstly checking that the actors are being faithful to the script, and secondly helping the actors out when they forget their lines. It is a difficult task, because it takes a certain amount of experience to know when to prompt a performer. Some actors will approximate their lines for a few rehearsals until they have really got the scene under their belts. In this instance, prompting may be more distracting than anything else, and may pressurise the actor into making more mistakes than ever.

The best rule to follow, and this should be established at the beginning of rehearsals, is that if an actor requires help, he or she will say 'prompt' in order to indicate that some assistance is needed. The stage manager should then deliver the appropriate line in a clear, measured voice. Attempting to be discreet about this is usually counter-productive, since it can be really off-putting if the stage manager's prompting is inaudible and the actor is required to ask for the prompt for a second time. In the case of a confident actor who never asks for help, but constantly paraphrases the lines, the DSM should make a note during the rehearsal of the lines which are approximate, and should then find a convenient moment to approach the actor in order to correct the lines. It is important, though, not to interrupt the flow of the rehearsal for minor script inaccuracies; it is best to talk to the actor in a coffee break or while the director is working with another member of the cast. Letting the actor get away with script changes will lead to general sloppiness and an inaccurate rendition of the piece, so it really is the DSM's duty to correct these mistakes as early as possible. After all, if an actor commits an inaccurate line to memory, and only becomes aware of the mistake at the dress rehearsal, it may be very difficult to revert back to the original text in time for the first public performance.

Once the production moves into the theatre, the actors will probably have to fend for themselves and manage without prompting. The fact is that the DSM will usually have far too much to think about in terms of cueing the show to be able to keep an eye on every line of the text as well. Prompting during the show is almost unheard of these days, and most actors have to rely on their fellow performers to throw them a line if they get into trouble.

Props

Before rehearsals begin it is a good idea for the stage manager to compile a provisional props list. This is very easily done by reading through the script and noting any props which are specified in the text. Of course, when it comes to rehearsals, the director may dispense with any or all of the suggestions in the script, and he or she will almost certainly want to add new props to the list as well. A provisional list is useful for several reasons; firstly because, as I mentioned in the previous chapter, rehearsal props should always be found to represent those items in the show which affect any part of an actor's performance, whether this be a pair of spectacles, an oil lantern, or a rifle, for example. The actual show prop may not appear until the dress rehearsal, but it is vitally important that the performers have something to work with up until this point. It is the stage manager's responsibility to ensure that rehearsal props are provided, even if in practise this only involves organising the actors to bring something suitable from home.

The list is also useful since it gives an indication of any unusual items which may need to be hired or specially made for the production, and the sooner the stage manager sets about organising this the better. For example, the script for *Oklahoma!* specifies that the first scene opens with Aunt Eller churning butter in an old wooden butter churn. This is the sort of obscure prop which may be difficult to locate, and a well-organised stage manager should check as soon as possible whether the director is likely to require this item, so that there is plenty of time to do something about it if it is needed.

So, as the rehearsals progress and the director, choreographer, and actors work out what will be needed for the show, the provisional props list will slowly mutate into the definitive list. Usually the designer will expect to be informed of all decisions concerning props, and in some cases he or she will take responsibility for actually tracking down the unusual items. Specialist prop hire companies are listed in *Contacts* (see appendix), but many props can be secured by begging and borrowing. Often local shops will help out in return for a mention in the programme, and it is always worth approaching other companies who have done productions of the same show. Some items, however, will simply be impossible to find through any course of action, and in this case, the prop will have to be specially made, sometimes by a member of the stage management team. A recent production of Sondheim's *Into the Woods* which I directed required a moveable white cow with a hinged jaw, which could 'eat' various articles, such as a red cape, an ear of corn, a strand of hair, and a golden slipper! Not surprisingly, this prop had to be specially made, and caused one poor stage manager several sleepless nights.

The prop-setting list

As rehearsals progress, a prop-setting list will need to be drawn up by a member of the stage management, usually the DSM. This list is a detailed account of the setting for each prop in the show. Some props will need 'presetting' – this means that they will be set on stage by a member of stage management before the show begins, or during a scene change; some props will be set offstage on a props table, and clearly marked so that the actors can take them prior to going on stage; and other props, called personal props will be preset in the actors' dressing-rooms – these tend to be items that the actors can carry, such as cigarette lighters, handkerchieves, spectacles, and wrist watches. Some show props will, of course, need replacing on a regular basis; these will include any food and drink which is consumed during the show, any fresh flowers that are used, and any items such as newspapers or letters which are likely to look tatty after several performances.

By the end of the rehearsal period there should be a definitive props list and a provisional prop-setting list. Of course, some aspects of prop-setting can only be finalised once the company has moved into the theatre, and the stage management team has had a chance to work out how best to use the backstage areas. Final decisions may have to wait until the technical rehearsals.

Sound effects

As rehearsals progress it will become increasingly clear which sound effects are going to be required for the show. The DSM (or whoever is running the prompt book) will be expected to note the specific cue points for each sound effect in the prompt copy. For most shows (with the exception of big-budget musicals which usually have a separate sound department) the job of finding these sound effects will usually fall to a member of the stage management team.

Fortunately there is an increasing number of sound-effects CDs on the market, and a bewildering array of different sounds to choose from. There are some sounds, however, which are very difficult to reproduce, and in certain circumstances a live effect will be more appropriate. The sound of gun-shot is a good example of this; it is much better to use a gun with blanks in, than to try to replicate the sound electronically. The sound of glass smashing is another effect which comes over as manufactured when recorded; where possible, it is better for a member of stage management to actually break some glass offstage to create the effect. Of course, great care must be taken when doing this, and it is usually best to make sure that the glass is broken inside a box, so that the noise can easily be heard by the audience, but there is no danger involved in the procedure.

Safety and time-keeping

The stage management team needs to place a great deal of emphasis upon safety in the rehearsal room. This means closely monitoring the work in progress, and informing the director if any stage action is likely to be potentially hazardous. It is not unheard of for a director to get carried away with the creative process, and to allow the actors to experiment with physical work which is actually beyond their capabilities, or which may simply be impossible to repeat night after night during the course of the run. A subtle word in the director's ear may just save an actor from being rushed into casualty with a broken limb.

It is also important for the stage management to monitor the number of hours that the actors are working. In professional theatre, of course, over-running in rehearsals has very obvious financial implications. But it is just as important to regulate the hours of a group of unpaid actors, and the stage management should try to ensure that the actors are given regular breaks, and that they are not expected to work ludicrous hours, especially during the final stages of rehearsals as the performance dates loom ever closer, and the atmosphere becomes increasingly tense.

Liaising with other members of the production team

A vital part of the stage manager's job is to make sure that any decisions that are reached during rehearsals are immediately reported back to the appropriate departments. If, while staging a number, the director decides to get an actor to climb a tree, or to leap onto a fence, for example, then it is most important that this information is reported back to the designer, so that these specific pieces of scenery can be reinforced in the workshop. There is nothing worse than reaching the dress rehearsal and discovering that half the things that have been staged in the rehearsal room are, in practice, impossible to achieve on the set.

Similarly, as far as lighting is concerned, if the director is clearly envisaging a stroboscopic effect at one point in the show, for example, it is important that the lighting designer knows this, and that he or she has time to order the specific equipment to achieve this effect. Of course, if there is good communication between the director and the other members of the creative team, this sort of problem should not arise; it is well worth the stage manager double-checking though, just in case. By acting as a go-between for the different departments, the stage manager can help to avoid misunderstandings, and to smooth over any breakdown in communications.

Production meetings

Communication between the various departments is really vital at this stage in the rehearsal process, and the stage manager should make it a priority to organise regular production meetings, so that representatives from each of the departments can meet and discuss the progress being made in their particular area of work. For those people whose work takes place mainly outside the rehearsal room, such as the set designer, the lighting designer, and the costume designer, these production meetings provide a good opportunity to 'touch base' and to find out what exactly has been going on in rehearsals. The producer should always try to be available for these meetings, because in my experience, recurring problems at this stage tend to be concerned with the budget, and the producer is really the only one who can help to sort out these concerns. Where possible, someone from stage management should always try to take the 'minutes' at these meetings, so that members of the production team who are unable to attend can at least read about the issues which have been discussed at the meeting.

Setting a technical schedule These meetings also provide a good opportunity for the various heads of department to discuss a provisional technical schedule for the show once the production moves into the theatre. The designer (with advice from the production manager or the set builder) should be able to estimate how long it will take to construct the set in the theatre, the lighting designer ought to be able to give a fairly accurate idea about the time it will take for the rigging and focusing of the lights, and if there is a sound designer working on the project, he or she should be able to assess the time that it will take to install all the necessary sound equipment, to check the levels, and to mix the sound. Once the director and the stage manager have been advised about these estimates, they should be able to organise a suitable schedule for the production week. This can then be presented to the others for approval at a later production meeting.

Liaising with the theatre personnel

During rehearsals, the stage manager will also need to liaise with the theatre front-of-house manager, assuming that there is one. He or she will want to know how many intervals there will be during the show, what the timings will be for each act, and when the performance is estimated to finish. Assuming that the production is being mounted in a theatre, these questions are all geared towards the employment of front-of-house staff, fire officers, stage-door keepers, etc. The front-of-house manager may also need to know specific details about the production, especially if the show is likely to include any of the following;

- loud bangs
- stroboscopic effects
- nudity
- strong language

The box-office staff will need to be informed about any of the above so that they can warn potential audience members about anything in the show that may cause discomfort or offence.

Wardrobe fittings and costume plots

During rehearsals the costume designer will need to have access to the performers in order to fit them for their costumes. If possible the stage manager should try to work out a schedule for this which dove-tails with the director's rehearsal schedule; any actor who is not being rehearsed by a member of the creative team should in theory be free to have a costume fitting. Where possible costume fittings should work around the rehearsal schedule, rather than interfering with it; in practice, though, this is not always possible. As I have mentioned earlier in the book, the costume designer may have a particularly difficult task since, unlike the set designer, much of his or her creative work is likely to be done during the rehearsals. For this reason, the stage management should try to ensure that the actors turn up promptly for these costume fittings, so that the costume designer can make maximum use of the time. Some performers may also need to be fitted for wigs; these fittings should also be arranged around the director's main schedule.

While liaising with the costume designer the stage manager should discuss any costume changes which may be difficult to achieve during the show, and should then warn the director of any potential problem areas before the first dress rehearsal. Some costume designers will devise a costume plot (see below) which provides a clear visual indication of the scenes in which each actor appears and the costume that he or she will be required to wear at specific points in the show. This costume plot can also help to pin-point the particular scenes where costume changes may potentially be difficult to achieve.

THE DEMON HEADMASTER — COSTUME PLOT

ACT 1

CHARACTER/CAST	SCENE 1	SCENE 2	SCENE 3	SCENE 4	SCENE 5	SCENE 6	SCENE 7	SCENE 8
DINAH LIZZIE RENIHAN		White school blouse Black pleated skirt Pink/blue/white jumper Black tights Black loafers		Same as scene 1	White school blouse Blue and gold tie Blue blazer Black pleated skirt Black tights Black loafers	Same as scene 5	Same as scene 5	Same as scene 5
LLOYD CHRIS JEFFERSON	Blue blazer White school shirt Blue and gold tie Black trousers Black socks Trainers		Same as scene 1	Same as scene 1	Same as scene 1		Same as scene 1	
HARVEY SAM KENYON	Blue blazer White school shirt Blue and gold tie Black trousers Black shoes Grey socks Yellow peaked cap	Same as scene 1	Same as scene 1	Same as scene 1	Same as scene 1		Same as scene 1	Same as scene 1
INGRID GAIL MACKINNON	Blue Blazer White school blouse Blue and gold tie Black pleated skirt White ankle socks Trainers Floral hair ties	Same as scene 1					Same as scene 1	

Other important stage management duties

While the production is in rehearsal, the stage manager will need to start thinking about organising the costume parade and the production photo call, which will both take place during production week, once the show has moved into the theatre. Depending upon the specific requirements of the piece, the stage manager (or in some cases, the producer) may also need to apply for a licence for one or more of the following:

Children The regulations concerning the appearance of children in theatrical productions are quite complicated, and in most cases a licence will need to be granted from the relevant local authority. This will allow the child or children to appear for a certain number of performances, and under certain specific conditions. If in doubt, the stage manager should contact the local council for details, preferably before rehearsals begin.

Firearms It is usually necessary to obtain a firearms certificate before being able to use a firing gun on stage. However, there are several types of weapon which fall outside this ruling, including starting pistols and replicas. There are also stringent rules which apply to the handling of guns in a theatre or theatrical venue, and it is absolutely forbidden to leave firing guns on props tables or generally lying about backstage. When not in use they should always be stored in a lockable safe, and when required for a scene they should be handed to the performer by a member of stage management just before they go on stage.

Fire The rules concerning naked flame on stage vary depending on the type of venue. Most theatres will have a fire officer who will need to be advised about the intended use of fire, and the smoking of cigarettes. If in doubt it is probably best to approach the relevant authorities for advice. Where permission is granted, the stage manager will need to take certain precautions to ensure that safety remains an absolute priority. For example, if cigarettes are used in a scene, there must be fire extinguishers in each wing, and ash trays should always have sand or water in them so that cigarettes are extinguished immediately, rather than being allowed to smoulder. Where pyrotechnical effects are being used, the stage manager must take extra precautions to ensure that any part of the set which stands nearby is thoroughly fire-proofed.

Animals Although I would generally say that one should avoid having animals on stage at all costs, there are several musicals which have very specific requirements, such as *The Wizard of Oz*, in which Dorothy really does need a four-legged friend. To use an animal on stage, a certificate should be obtained from the relevant authorities. It is also very important when using live animals to make sure that they are well treated on and off stage. Quite apart from anything else, if the audience perceives that an animal is unhappy on stage, there is certain to be a stream of angry letters to the director.

Special effects

Musicals often include some fantastical or magical elements, and on balance are more likely to require 'special effects' than a straight play. I don't intend to dwell on this particular speciality in this book, but it is worth pointing out that any special effects which are required for a show must be planned well in advance. While the director and the set designer will probably come up with the ideas, it usually falls to the lighting designer to make them a reality, and it will often be the responsibility of the stage management to operate and maintain the necessary equipment. Smoke and fog effects can be very atmospheric, and many a dream ballet has been enhanced by the addition of swirling clouds of dry ice. Unfortunately there is little point in trying out these effects in the rehearsal room, since smoke and dry ice are fairly temperamental, and will react very differently in different locations, depending upon temperature and air flow. However, once in the theatre, the stage management should try to find time to experiment with these effects, ideally before the actors arrive on the set. Explosions and other pyrotechnical effects should also be tested prior to the tech run, but only when the set has been thoroughly fire-proofed.

It is well worth remembering that there are many wonderful effects that the lighting designer can create just by the use of light alone. By adjusting the light behind a gauze (or scrim) for example, actors can be made to appear and disappear in the blink of an eye. Gobbos (patterned templates which are placed in front of the light source) can also give a stunning effect, and are relatively cheap to use.

As I mentioned in the previous chapter, magic tricks will often require the assistance of a specialist, and if the show needs any flying effects, there are several companies which deal exclusively with this speciality (see the Props and Trades section of *Contacts*). It is important to remember, however, that this sort of stage trickery requires a fair amount of planning, a lot of technical time in the theatre, and a sizeable budget.

Final runs in the rehearsal room

As the rehearsals progress, the prompt book will gradually start to fill up with vital pieces of information concerning sound cues, provisional lighting cues, blocking for the actors, props lists, etc. By the final week of rehearsals, the production should be starting to settle into some sort of shape, and what seemed like an untameable beast in the first few days of rehearsals should begin to appear much more manageable now. Of course, there are still many hurdles to leap before the show will be ready for an audience, but by this stage in rehearsals, the actors, and the stage management should all be pretty clear about the particular nature of the show, and will be fully aware of the potential problems. At this stage props lists can begin to be finalised, and prop-setting lists should be as accurate as they can be, given that changes will inevitably occur once the show transfers into the theatre.

In my skeleton rehearsal schedule (see p.70) I suggested that for a musical with four weeks of allocated rehearsal time, the aim should be to have three full run-throughs at the end of the final week. In practice, of course, this may not always happen, and sometimes due to time pressures the first full run-through occurs at the dress rehearsal stage. This situation should really be avoided if possible, since it throws everyone into a panic; the cast, the production team, and the stage management alike. Running the show several times in the rehearsal room gives everyone the chance to get to grips with the piece, and also helps to build some much-needed confidence before having to face the daunting, and often difficult process of 'teching' and 'dressing' the show (see Chapter 11).

Before embarking upon one of these final run-throughs, it is a good idea to get the cast in the mood by having a short dance warm-up, a vocal recap of some of the ensemble numbers, or a few well-chosen theatre games. The important thing is to get the cast thinking and working together, and any exercises that will help to achieve this are useful at this stage. Some directors will find time to do a 'speed run' of all the spoken dialogue in the show. This is basically a run-through of all the scenes at speed, usually without any of the blocking or actions. Personally I don't find this approach particularly useful, and I tend to think that if the actors are still shaky on the script at this point in rehearsals, then a speed run is hardly likely to cement the lines anyway.

It is best to treat these run-throughs as performances, so that the actors and the stage management can start to see the show as a whole, and can begin to focus on logistical matters, such as the length of time available to do costume and scene changes. If the actors are under the impression that they can 'mark through' the run, i.e. go through the motions of the piece rather than immersing themselves in it, the run-through is likely to be under-energised and unfocused, and will consequently be of little value to the cast, the stage management, or the production team. On the other hand, a run at performance level should get everyone's adrenalin going, and will start to give the whole team a clearer idea of the show's potential.

Costume and props

For these runs, the stage management should ensure that the rehearsal room is as uncluttered as possible, and that the only items on or near the stage area are the props and the set-dressing. If it is possible to use the show props, rather than those that have been used for rehearsal purposes, so much the better. Likewise, if any of the costumes are ready and available, it will certainly benefit the actors to try wearing them during these runs. In many cases, costumes will have to be altered once the actors have tried working in them, and the sooner the costume department is made aware of any problems, the sooner they can start to do the necessary alterations.

If the costumes are not available to be worn at this stage, the actors should be encouraged to find suitable alternatives, so that their outfit for these runs is an approximation of their show costume. This may mean the men bringing in a shirt and tie, for example, or the women wearing a skirt or a dress. Where dance is concerned, it is particularly important for the performers to try out their show shoes as soon as possible, and ideally they should begin to practise in the correct footwear during the rehearsal period. Again, if this is left to the last minute, and the dancers start to discover problems with their footwear during the final dress rehearsal, it could have serious repercussions for the show, and will certainly cause a lot of unnecessary angst for the performers and for the costume department.

Bringing it all together

The stage manager should make absolutely certain that the run-throughs are being timed, since the box office will need to know running times for each act as soon as possible so that they can inform the public about interval times, and give an estimated timing for the end of the show. It is customary, also, to give some indication of running times in the programme, and the sooner this information is made available the better.

The personnel present at each run-through will depend to a certain extent upon how many runs are likely to take place. Ideally the lighting designer should try to attend as many runs as possible, and should always try to sit next to the director so that they can discuss the lighting cues while the rehearsal is in progress. If the show requires the use of manually operated spotlights (follow spots), the operators should also attend a couple of rehearsal room runs. Ideally they should be given scripts at this point, and advised about provisional cue points. Of course, things are bound to change in the theatre, but if this preparation has been done already, a lot of technical rehearsal time can be saved.

Assuming that there is a sound designer involved in the project, he or she should certainly attend a couple of these runs, so that the specific vocal dynamics of the show can be assessed before having to worry about the accoustics of the theatre and the problems involved in amplifying the orchestra or band. Obviously the director will be present during these runs, and with shows which involve complicated movement or dance, the choreograper should also be in attendance. In most cases the musical director will also be the conductor of the show, but where finances are limited, he or she may in fact be leading the band from the keyboard. Whatever the circumstances, whoever will be conducting or leading the band for the first public performances of the show should certainly do so for these last few runs.

The stage manager will be expected to control the rehearsal room for these final run-throughs, and while the DSM will be concentrating on the prompt book, and checking cue points, the stage manager will take responsibility for starting and stopping the rehearsal, and for ensuring that the run is well organised and efficiently managed. The cast will quickly adjust to the stage management activity around them, and will soon get used to a certain person handing them a prop, or a particular member of the team moving the stage furniture.

Although in performance it is often the case that the stage management personnel will change from time to time (especially during long runs), the team which is in place during these final rehearsal runs should be the same as that working on the opening night. This continuity will not only help to make the show run as smoothly as possible, but it will also benefit the actors, who will feel much more comfortable surrounded by specific people doing familiar things at a particular point in the show.

Note sessions

After the run it is always a good idea for the creative team to give notes while the performance is still fresh in everybody's mind. A scrappy or unfocused run can be very upsetting for everyone involved, but it is important, I think, for the director to remember that these initial run-throughs, conducted under the critical gaze of the production team, can be very unnerving for both the performers and the stage management. Positive encouragement can be vital at this point, and it pays to temper any critical notes with one or two words of praise.

Ideally there should be time for each member of the creative team to give their own specific notes, and often the stage manager will also want to talk through some of the technical problems encountered during the run. Sometimes, especially where musical staging and dance are concerned, it is better to get the actors up on their feet and to work through the notes physically. However, if the performers have been working all day and have just completed a run of the show, they may be unresponsive to this sort of detailed work. In such cases, it is best to sit them down, give them a few well-chosen notes, and save the rest until the following morning.

A final word on giving notes; in my experience, most actors are sensitive creatures, and respond well to positive encouragement. While the actors playing the leading roles will usually receive a fair amount of attention from the production team, and will no doubt have to deal with some positive and some negative comments, it is very often the case that the ensemble get completely forgotten about, or receive very general notes about their group performance, as opposed to anything more individual and specific. I try, where possible, to find a time in rehearsals to talk to each performer, irrespective of the size of their role, and to try to pick out positive things to say about their performance. Ensemble

Giving notes to the cast of *Closer Than Ever* (PHOTO: Ashley Straw)

members are often surprised (and I suspect pleased) to find that their particular contribution has been noticed at all, and as soon as they start to feel that they have something valuable to offer to the production, their sense of commitment invariably improves. No one likes to think of themselves as an insignificant cog in a vast machine, and allowing a performer to take pride in his or her contribution can have very positive results for the production as a whole.

After the final run has taken place, the whole production will now move lock, stock and barrel into the theatre or performance venue. As soon as the actors have gone, the stage manager needs to ensure that the rehearsal room is returned to its original state; this will involve pulling up the tape from the marked-out floor, and removing all the paraphernalia that has built up in the room during rehearsals. Any show props and costumes which have been used during the final runs should be carefully packed away, and immediately transported to the theatre.

Leaving the rehearsal room for the last time is a strange experience for all concerned. This has been home to the company for a number of weeks, and assuming that the rehearsals have gone well, many exciting discoveries will have been made there, and much fun will have been had in the making. Moving into the theatre often seems to be a daunting prospect at this stage, partly because the security of the rehearsal room is about to be given up, but mainly because the rehearsal process is nearing its end, and the prospect of the first public performance is starting to loom large on the horizon.

Before moving to the theatre or performance space, most musical theatre productions will need to have a 'sitzprobe'. This rather forbidding word actually describes one of the most exciting moments in the whole process. It refers to the rehearsal in which the band (or orchestra) and the performers come together for the first time. Prior to the sitzprobe, the musicians will usually have had several rehearsals with the musical director and should be fairly familiar with the score by this stage. This rehearsal is entirely geared towards the music, and the performers will not be required to dance, or to move, and the only dialogue that they will be expected to perform will either be a cue into a musical number, or a section of script which is underscored by the band.

The purpose of the sitzprobe is to work through the entire score with both the cast and the musicians, focusing upon any sections which are complicated or unclear for either group. It usually takes place after the final run-through in the rehearsal room, and before the show moves into the theatre. The stage management will need to liaise with the musical director about organising the sitzprobe, and there are one or two points which they should all take into consideration:

- The rehearsal room used for this purpose should be large enough to seat the whole band and the entire cast, not to mention the director and several other members of the production team.

- Music stands will need to be supplied for the musicians, and assuming that a piano is required (it usually is), the stage management need to check that it has recently been tuned.

- Depending on the size of the band, amplification for the singers may need to be supplied. This is mainly to stop the performers over-singing, which at this late stage in the rehearsal process could be disastrous. It is not usually necessary to have individual mikes for all the performers, but there should be enough so that whenever a group of soloists are singing together, they can each use a separate microphone.

- Ideally the sitzprobe should take place in a room which is well sound-proofed so that the rehearsal is not compromised by noise from outside. Rooms which are very resonant and have a noticeable echo are also not a good idea, for obvious reasons.

The sitzprobe is often the only time that the performers will ever hear the band as it is supposed to sound. From this point onwards, the musicians are likely to be tucked away in an orchestra pit below the actors' feet, squashed into a corner of the wings, or in some cases, hidden away in a separate room. The subtlety of the orchestrations is often very hard to appreciate under such circumstances, and for this reason the whole cast should be encouraged to attend this rehearsal, even if there are some performers who don't actually sing in the show.

The sitzprobe can be a glorious experience, and often feels like a real landmark on the journey towards the opening night. It may also be the last opportunity for the cast to concentrate solely on the music; from now on the technicalities of the show will take precedence, and once in the theatre the actors will be inundated with problems of a comparatively uncreative nature, such as ill-fitting costumes, over-crowded dressing-rooms, wobbly sets, and foul-tempered directors. In my experience, the sitzprobe is often the calm before the storm, and the actors should be encouraged to savour the experience accordingly.

The musical director and double-bass player during the sitzprobe of *Closer Than Ever* (PHOTO: Ashley Straw)

11 · From the rehearsal room to the stage

Production week

The period between leaving the rehearsal space and opening the show to the public is called the 'production week', irrespective of how many days this actually takes. During this time there is a bewildering amount to achieve, and for this reason there must be very careful planning to ensure that the time is used as productively as possible. During the production meetings, which should ideally have taken place at regular intervals during rehearsals, the director and stage manager should have drawn up a detailed schedule for this production week, and cleared it with each of the heads of department. The production schedule illustrated on p.27 shows the allocation of time for technical and dress rehearsals once the actors have arrived in the theatre. Similarly, the stage manager must ensure that a detailed production schedule is drawn up to cover the period prior to this, when the 'get-in' and the 'fit-up' will need to take place.

The get-in and the fit-up
The get-in refers to the process of bringing the necessary equipment into the theatre and positioning it ready for use; this equipment includes the set, the props, the lighting, the sound system, and the costumes. The fit-up is the process of constructing the set, rigging the lights, wiring up the sound system, and generally preparing the theatre so that when the actors arrive, the technical rehearsals can begin without delay. This period of preparation requires skilful and detailed planning by the stage manager, since there is a great deal to achieve at this point, and, literally, no time to lose.

Colour and light

From early on in design meetings, the lighting designer will begin to devise a provisional lighting plot for the show. However, unlike the job of the set designer, and to some extent the costume designer, he or she will be forced to make creative decisions fairly late in the whole process, since it is only possible to think in general terms about lighting effects until the cast and director have had a chance to explore the show in rehearsals. The lighting designer will try to keep abreast of the progress in the rehearsal room and will be in close communication with the director during this time, but he or she can really only begin to work out the specific details of the lighting plot once the show has been blocked and the actors have had a chance to run the piece in its entirety. In most cases this only occurs towards the end of the rehearsal period. In some ways, lighting designers have the hardest job of all, since they have a very limited amount of time to assess the specific needs of the show. Also, as they are constantly compromised by tight schedules, they have little time to experiment and to make mistakes.

During rehearsals the director will usually begin to envisage certain lighting effects which will help to enhance the look of the show and will create a specific atmosphere for each scene. As a director I find that if I can communicate these visual ideas to the lighting designer, he or she will not only have a clearer idea about my intentions for a scene, but will also have a starting point from which to

A member of stage management adjusts a lantern during a focusing session (PHOTO: Ashley Straw)

work. Of course, the lighting designer may choose to develop these ideas, or to jettison them completely, but at least there will have been a communication of creative ideas.

Towards the end of the rehearsals I usually give the lighting designer a marked-up script detailing the sort of effects I had in mind when rehearsing the scene, and also the cue points where I imagine lighting changes may occur. The lighting designer can then watch a run-through with my provisional lighting plan as a rough guide. From this point on, with a much clearer idea of the blocking and the director's intentions, he or she can begin to develop a more detailed lighting plot for the show. This will only become the definitive plot once the lighting designer has had a chance to experiment during the technical rehearsals, and to see the actual actors, costumed and made up, and going through their blocking on the set.

Focusing and plotting

Once the get-in and the fit-up have been completed and the lights have been positioned and secured according to the rigging plan that has previously been devised, the lighting designer will need to start focusing each lantern so that light is shed on exactly the right areas of the stage (see photo on p.110). Ideally, by the time this occurs the stage should have been painted, the correct stage furniture should be in position, and there should be complete darkness on stage except for the lamps actually being focused. Once this process is completed, the lighting designer, much like a painter, will have a varied palette to choose from, and will now be able to isolate the lights, mix them together, or change their intensities as required. This is where the lighting designer can really begin to flex his or her creative muscles.

The director may or may not be present during this preliminary lighting session, but by the time the first technical rehearsal begins, the lighting designer should have plenty of ideas to show the director, and may even have preplotted some of the lighting states already.

Sound checks

Just as the lights require focusing before any plotting can be done, in a similar way the sound designer will need to set provisional sound levels and check the positioning of the effects loud speakers before the technical rehearsals begin. For a show which involves a complicated sound system, especially a musical which requires each actor to have a personal body mike, these early sound checks will need to be much more extensive. Also, for a show which requires a large band or orchestra, there will need to be specific balancing sessions to enable the sound designer to adjust the levels of sound according to the acoustic of the building and the nature of each instrument. Since the sound designer or sound operator will need absolute silence in the theatre to set levels, it is usually a good idea to

A member of stage management adjusts the sound levels during a technical rehearsal (PHOTO: Ashley Straw)

organise the sound check during a lunch break while members of the other departments are out of the building.

Actors in the theatre

Once the actors arrive in the theatre, they will need to be shown to their dressing rooms. In most cases the stage manager will organise the dressing room allocation, usually reserving single rooms for the principal actors, and placing the male and female ensembles in larger, separate rooms. If the theatre or performance space is an unknown venue to most of the cast, the stage manager should make sure that everyone is shown around the building. Not only should they all know how to get from the dressing rooms to the stage, and from stage right to stage left without crossing the stage, they should also be shown the fire exits in case of emergency.

Most theatres or theatrical venues will have some sort of Tannoy system which enables the stage manager to contact the cast from one centralised location. Usually there is also provision for a show relay, which means that during the performance everyone in the dressing rooms can hear what is happening on stage. This show relay will cut out when the stage manager needs to make an announcement.

It is usually best to stipulate to the cast that no one should venture on stage until they are given permission by the stage manager. At this point there are always a

The set for *Closer Than Ever* at the Jermyn Street Theatre (PHOTO: Ashley Straw)

million things going on, such as fixing lights, painting the set, and setting the stage furniture, and actors will only get in the way if they are allowed to wander freely over the set. While the actors are familiarising themselves with the theatre, the director and the choreographer should make sure that they have time to go out into the auditorium and check the sight-lines. However accurate a model box may be, there will always be some surprises when the production moves into the theatre. As long as the director recognises any sight-line problems at an early stage, he or she can easily reblock accordingly during the technical rehearsal. It is a good idea to suggest that the actors explore the auditorium as well, since it will give them a much clearer idea about the space that they are working in.

The stage manager will usually set up the production desk in the middle of the auditorium towards the back of the stalls. This is the place where the director and the DSM will sit during the tech. Usually the lighting designer will sit with them, so that he or she can discuss the lighting states with the director, and can check cue points with the DSM.

Costume parade

The costume parade usually takes place on stage at the theatre, some time before the technical rehearsals begin. It provides an opportunity for the director and costume designer to see all the actors wearing their particular costume or costumes, preferably in a lighting state from the show itself. If the lighting department are still focusing at this point, they may be able to provide an approximate state just for the costume parade. As with the sound check, a suitable time for this parade is a lunch-break when most of the technical staff will be out of the auditorium.

Sometimes the production schedule will be so tight that it is simply not possible to spare the necessary stage time for this costume viewing, and in such cases the stage management should organise an alternative venue. Once the costumes have been approved by the director, and the actors have had a chance to check that they can dance or move appropriately in their particular outfits, the costume designer can finally breathe a huge sigh of relief and start to worry about what he or she is going to wear to the opening night party.

Placing call

At some stage during the technical rehearsals, the choreographer will probably want to do a 'placing call'; this simply means working through the dance sections with the actors on stage, using the appropriate set dressings and props. Depending upon the show and the nature of the choreography, this rehearsal can often take place during a lunch-break, but it is most important that the actors involved in this call are given adequate time for a break at a later stage.

Fitting in a placing call before the technical rehearsals begin is a luxury that should be welcomed by the choreographer, since it provides the option of working through the danced sections of the show at a reasonable pace, without having the rest of the company standing by waiting for the technical rehearsal to resume. For this call, the choreographer should liaise with the costume department so that everyone involved is able to wear their show footwear, and ideally any articles of clothing which may cause movement problems, such as crinolines, long dresses, and corsets.

A member of stage management sweeps the stage before the technical rehearsal begins (PHOTO: Ashley Straw)

Technical rehearsals

The technical rehearsal is essentially a stopping run-through which incorporates every technical aspect of the show, including sound, lighting, special effects, scenery, props, and costumes. By the end of this detailed rehearsal, all these various strands of the show should have been pulled together, and the actors should be clear about all aspects of staging, and confident about entrances and exits, finding and using props, and doing quick changes. For a musical production there should always be a pianist for the technical rehearsal. This accompanist does not necessarily need to be the musical director (in fact it is probably better for the MD to conduct the show during this rehearsal), but he or she should be very familiar with the score, and should at least have played for some of the rehearsals.

Although every technical rehearsal will differ in some way from the next, the basic set-up is usually pretty similar. The director will sit at the production desk with the DSM and the lighting designer, while the stage manager will be mobile, usually in the wings or on the stage itself. Communication between the stage manager and the various other departments will normally be via head-sets (or 'cans'). In larger venues, a 'God mike' will often be provided for the director, so that any instructions can be heard clearly by the whole company.

The director will sometimes need to go up onto the stage to sort out a specific problem; this may occasionally be unavoidable, but with regard to staging, it is probably better to ask the choreographer to help out, and for the director to remain in the auditorium. It may seem an insignificant detail, but if the company has to wait for the director to return to the production desk every time he or she hops up on stage, a lot of useful technical time can be wasted. The director is able to be more objective from out in the auditorium, and is also able to restart the rehearsal at a moment's notice.

Lighting cues

In an ideal world, the lighting designer will have preplotted most of the lighting cues, and will simply need to tweak them during the tech. In practice, however, this is hardly ever the case, since the get-in and fit-up are usually very tight, and the lighting designer often has a difficult job simply finishing the focusing before the technical rehearsal begins. In this case, he or she will actually be plotting lighting states as the rehearsal progresses, and often the stage manager will have to stop the action in order to wait for the lighting department. Once the lighting designer is happy with a cue, the DSM will note it in the prompt book, and the cue will be recorded by the board operator. Most modern theatres use computerised lighting boards, which means that this process is fairly swift, but some venues still use a manual board, and this can be much slower.

Running the rehearsal

It usually saves time during the run if the stage manager allows a few minutes before the tech begins to take the cast around the set, highlighting any potential problem areas such as staircases and trap-doors, and even seemingly simple things like window catches and door handles. The cast will always feel more comfortable once this familiarisation process has taken place. After all, the stage will effectively be home to the actors for some time to come, and it is important that they should start to get used to it as soon as possible.

Just before starting the tech, it is useful for the director to address the assembled company, and to explain in brief how the ensuing rehearsal will progress. It is customary for the stage manager to be in charge of this technical rehearsal, although in practice the authority is often split between the stage manager and the director. In my experience it is the director who stops the run in order to sort out a lighting state, a sound cue, or a piece of blocking, but it is the stage manager who will call for the continuation of the rehearsal. If something dangerous is about to happen on the other hand, such as the possibility of falling scenery or a run-away scenic truck, the stage manager should immediately take control and stop the run. However the director and stage manager wish to control this rehearsal, the situation needs to be clarified to the rest of the company before the run begins.

Although professional actors will be well aware of the nature of a technical rehearsal, it will certainly be worth the director pointing out to an amateur cast that this rehearsal is not for the purposes of characterisation or motivation. In fact the technical rehearsals are really only concerned with practicalities relating to scenery, costumes, props, effects, lighting, and sound. Both the director and the actors should be concentrating on all things technical, and the former should try to avoid giving character notes at this point. As far as singing is concerned, the cast will obviously want to get used to the acoustics in the theatre, and if personal radio mikes are being used, the sound department will sometimes need to hear the voices singing full out. But the cast must remember that due to the nature of the technical rehearsal, they are likely to have to repeat sections of the show a number of times, and should therefore be very careful about over-singing at this crucial stage in the process.

Scene changes and special effects

Depending upon the nature of the show and the complexity of the design, it sometimes makes sense for the stage manager to organise a scene change rehearsal before the actors arrive on the set. This really only makes sense if the scene changes are automated, or if they are handled exclusively by the stage management and crew. If any of the actors are required to assist (and it is becoming increasingly acceptable for actors to change sets in full view of the audience), then there is really no point in trying to rehearse the change without everyone in attendance.

Occasionally a show will require a specific stage action or stage effect which needs rehearsing before the actors appear. It is certainly a good idea to try out smoke effects, explosions and flashes before the cast arrive, and it is also worth looking ahead to see if any other potential problems can be solved prior to the technical rehearsal. On a recent production of *Jesus Christ Superstar*, for example, the scene in which Jesus is nailed to the cross was first rehearsed with stage management only, since it involved attaching someone to the cross before raising it to its upright position, a potentially dangerous manoeuvre. Once the move was perfected by the stage management, the actor playing Jesus was called in to watch, and was subsequently rehearsed into the action. This was all done calmly and efficiently before the technical rehearsal, so that the actor felt entirely comfortable and safe when it came to 'teching' this section of the show with full lighting and sound.

Making full use of the time

In my experience, all technical rehearsals have several things in common; firstly there is never enough time, and the process always feels pressurised. This means that there is a certain amount of tension in all departments, and it is very easy for tempers to flare up. The director and the stage manager should work together to keep the rehearsal calm and productive; any loss of temper from either person can be perceived as a lack of control, and control is one of the key priorities at this particular stage in the whole process.

Something else which is common to all technical rehearsals is boredom. While the director, the lighting designer, the DSM and the stage manager will need to be firing on all cylinders throughout this rehearsal, there will inevitably be times when the actors, and some of the stage management and crew, are waiting around doing nothing, sometimes for a very long time. The director should point out to the actors beforehand that these periods of inactivity can actually be used to their advantage; they can quietly go over scenes with their fellow actors, experiment with a prop which they have only just received, or practise dance steps at the side of the stage. As long as they are ready at a moment's notice to resume the rehearsal, they should really be able to use this time sensibly and productively.

Because time is always limited during the technical rehearsals, the real skill comes in being able to make maximum use of the available time. If, for example, everything suddenly grinds to a halt as the sound department has to start moving microphones around, there are plenty of other things that can be achieved during the hiatus. This would be a good opportunity for the choreographer to leap up on stage and clarify the positioning for one of the dance numbers, for example, or for the musical director to go over some harmony lines with the ensemble. As soon as the stage manager is ready to continue with the tech, however, everyone should be ready to resume the rehearsal immediately.

'Topping and tailing' Although in an ideal world the technical rehearsal would involve running through the whole musical from start to finish, often the pressures of time will force the director to 'top and tail' scenes from the show.

This means that various bits of dialogue, and sometimes whole sections of music, will be omitted so that valuable time can be saved. If a director is going to do this, it is absolutely vital that he or she checks to make sure that there are no lighting cues, sound cues, costume changes, or complicated bits of stage business within the omitted section of text or music. Much time will be wasted if the director suddenly realises after the event that a cue has been skipped, or that a costume change has been forgotten about.

Costume changes On the subject of costume changes, where possible, any difficult changes should be rehearsed prior to the technical rehearsal. Quick changes are often a complete nightmare to begin with, but what seems impossible is usually quite achievable once the actors know exactly what they are doing. Assuming that the quick change has been practised already, the director should make certain that it is possible in the context of the scene. Once the quick change has started, the dialogue or song which occurs at the same time should be continued until the actor reappears on stage in his or her new costume. Any interruption during this time will, of course, alter the timing of the scene and invalidate the procedure.

Technical rehearsals are, to my mind, a bit like going to the dentist; the prospect is fairly daunting, but the actual experience is usually less painful than expected. Where there is good communication between the separate departments, thoughtful preparation, and a calm but productive atmosphere, a huge amount can be achieved in a relatively short space of time. Other priorities include regular tea breaks (essential, since the theatre is a dangerous place, and tiredness and overwork can very easily lead to errors of judgement); a good sense of humour (vital at this taxing stage in the whole process) and a large supply of chocolate! The last remark is actually only half in jest, since it is often the case that the director, stage manager, lighting designer, and DSM spend their breaks going over some detail from the rehearsal, or trying to anticipate future problems. A proper lunch break is a real luxury, so it is always best to stock up with food, just in case there are no opportunities to leave the production desk once rehearsals start.

The photo call

Most producers will budget for a production photographer to come to the theatre and take pictures of the show. These photos can be used for publicity purposes in a number of different ways: they can be included in a press pack for journalists who come to review the show; they can be sent directly to local newspapers, preferably accompanied by some interesting facts or stories surrounding the piece; and they can be used as part of a front-of-house display. Production photographs are normally taken during the production week, although occasionally the photographer will also be asked to attend some rehearsals prior to this, so that interesting shots of the show can be developed and used for publicity purposes well before the production actually opens.

Organising the shoot

The stage manager should take responsibility for liaising with the production photographer and for organising the actual shoot. Some photographers prefer to take pictures during the dress rehearsal, since in this way the photos usually end up looking less 'stagey' and more spontaneous than prearranged shots. However, under subtle stage lighting photographic definition sometimes suffers, and it can be necessary to set up a special photo shoot, and to organise the stage lighting so that it is brighter than normal. In this case, the director (or photographer) will usually decide which moments from the show will make strong, eye-catching photographs. It is very unwise to attempt to shoot a particular shot simply by freezing the actors in one position, since the only way to ensure spontaneity in the photos is to try to capture the moment during a run of the specific scene.

It is always best to be well prepared for these photo shoots, since they often come at a time when the last thing on the director's mind is the photos for the front-of-house display. In my experience, time is always running short at this point in the process, and in order to lose as little time as possible over the photo shoot, I try to organise this session as meticulously as possible. There are several things to bear in mind, as far as the show photos are concerned:

A publicity photo taken during the dress rehearsal of *The Demon Headmaster*

1 Decide in advance which moments from the show are likely to make good photographs.

2 Make a running order of shots and allow the actors to see it in advance so that everyone has some idea when he or she will be needed, and in what costume. Make sure that the stage manager also has a copy of this. Always take into account costume changes for the actors, and try to make sure that at no point in the shoot is the photographer waiting around for someone to change into their next costume.

3 Make sure that the running order does not require too many scene changes, since it will slow everything down if stage management are constantly having to move the set.

4 Don't be over-ambitious; there is no point in trying to capture every moment from the show. Realistically, the front-of-house display is unlikely to need more than ten to fifteen shots, so concentrate on getting the photographer to shoot a certain number of scenes in careful detail, rather than going for broke and trying to cover everything.

The dress rehearsal

From the very first day of rehearsal, when the show is really only a collection of ideas in several peoples' heads, the musical starts to take shape, to develop, and to grow. As the rehearsals progress, new elements are added, such as props and various bits of costume. Once the musical reaches the theatre it changes once again, as several new layers are added; the lighting, the sound, and the scenery. At the dress rehearsal, when the actors will finally be fully costumed, all the disparate elements finally come together for the first time. Despite careful planning in every department, nobody really knows quite how the show will turn out once all the component parts slot into place. This is what makes the dress rehearsal both horribly nerve-wracking, and tremendously exciting.

Before the dress rehearsal begins, the stage management, crew, lighting department, sound department, and wardrobe will no doubt be racing around, madly trying to fix any problems which became apparent during the technical rehearsals. The DSM will be tidying up the prompt book and making sure that the cues are all absolutely clear, the designer will probably be doing some last minute painting on the set, and various actors will be running through their lines or agonising over dance steps and harmonies.

This point in the rehearsal process is somewhat disorienting for the actors. They have probably been rehearsing the show for three or four weeks (longer, of course, if the show has been rehearsed only a couple of times a week, as is often the case with school or community productions) and have by now become thoroughly immersed in the project. Since the technical rehearsals usually span

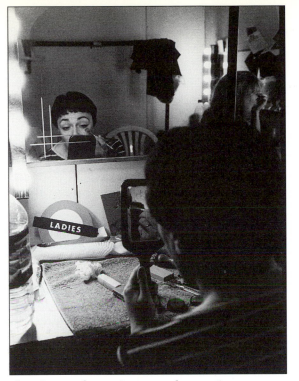

The dress rehearsal approaches and an actress prepares (PHOTO: Ashley Straw)

several days at the very least, the actors will not have actually run the piece without stopping for quite some time. They may all be starting to feel that they have lost touch with the show, and that the momentum gained in the final few days in the rehearsal room has completely evaporated. This feeling is absolutely normal and will, in most cases, disapppear once the dress rehearsal is under way. It may be useful for the director to gather the cast together before the dress rehearsal begins, just to help remind the actors that they are a united team, all striving towards the same ends. If there is time, which in truth there seldom is, the musical director may want to give the actors a quick warm-up, not so much to get their voices in shape, but more as a means of focusing the company's energies.

A professional approach

The only real difference between a dress rehearsal and a performance is that the former takes place in front of a nearly empty auditorium, and the latter is performed in front of a paying audience. The point is that every department should take this rehearsal as seriously as they would do a performance. The aim should be to run the show without stopping in as professional a manner as possible. Ideally the production desk should now be removed from the auditorium, and the actors should be asked to remain backstage when they are not in a scene (as opposed to sneaking into the theatre to watch bits of the show). The actors should be given the same calls as for a normal performance, and they should be expected to be in their dressing-rooms by the 'half', i.e., thirty-five minutes before the show begins. The actors will probably need all this time to change into their first act costumes, and to experiment with hair and make-up.

Make-up and wigs

In most circumstances make-up is supplied by the actor rather than by the production company, although for shows which involve complicated stage make-up such as *Cats* or *Starlight Express*, specialist make-up will usually be provided. Due to the sophisticated nature of stage lighting in contemporary theatre, applying stage make-up is no longer the complicated, time-consuming procedure that it used to be. In the past theatrical lighting often caused the actors' faces to appear washed out and make-up was applied liberally to compensate for this. Contemporary lighting is far more subtle, and in my experience make-up can usually be kept to a minimum. Where complicated make-up is required, it is a good idea to have someone on hand to deal with this, particularly for the first few performances while the actors are becoming more familiar with the process. Likewise, with shows requiring a number of wigs or hair-pieces (especially where these are required to have a 'period' look) there should be an experienced person on call to supervise the wearing of these accessories. This will usually be the wig master or mistress, but on smaller productions the costume designer may have to add this to his or her list of responsibilities.

And so at last the musical can be run in its entirety, with every element of the show in place. This will often be the first time that the cast and band have been together since the sitzprobe, and this additional musical element will give the show a whole new dimension. Once the musicians are tuned up and ready to play, and the production team are sitting in the auditorium nervously clutching their note-pads, the DSM can cue the house lights down and the dress rehearsal can begin. Ideally this rehearsal is run from start to finish without a break (except, of course, for the interval, which should be the same length as in performance), but if problems occur with a scene change, or something dangerous happens which could injure a member of the cast or the backstage team, then the stage manager will stop the run and attempt to sort out the problem.

Notes

Depending upon the finishing time for the dress rehearsal, the production team may wish to give notes after the performance. It is best to give the cast members a break immediately after the run, to give them time to change out of their costumes, remove their make-up, and have a drink. This may be a good opportunity for the director and stage manager to give technical notes to the various heads of department before the cast arrive to receive their notes. It is important to remember that the cast will have had a lot to take on board during the dress rehearsal, and, in my experience, it is best to leave detailed character notes to one side, since negative comments at this stage can lead to unnecessary anxiety in the actors – hardly ideal when facing an opening night performance. This is less important where there are several previews, since the cast will expect to continue experimenting and developing their characters during this time.

Previews

The concept of previews may seem terribly grand, since it tends to suggest large budgets and long runs. Actually it is becoming increasingly accepted, even with fringe shows, that a few performances in front of an audience can help to iron out any teething problems before the opening night. There is no doubt that a show changes dramatically once there is an audience watching it, and no matter how much detailed rehearsal has taken place, it is impossible to know beforehand quite how an audience will react to it. Perhaps there will be a spontaneous burst of applause after a particular song which no one was expecting, or maybe a scripted gag which in rehearsals had everyone on the floor with laughter will raise only a titter in performance. Audience reaction will inevitably have an effect upon the actors, and their performances will no doubt alter to some extent to accommodate this audience response.

As far as the production team is concerned, previews are a real godsend, since they give everyone the chance to tidy up any problems which may have been left over from the technical and dress rehearsals. It should be remembered, however, that the preview audience will have paid to see the show (although the ticket prices are usually reduced), and the production team should not regard these performances simply as a few extra dress rehearsals. The audience may expect one or two hiccups, but they deserve, nonetheless, to see a good professional show.

Bows and curtain calls

There is an old theatrical tradition that dictates that curtain calls should not be rehearsed until the day of the first performance. This is a superstition which I am more than happy to ignore. However, it is often the case that the curtain call is the last thing on anyone's mind, and will often get left until the eleventh hour anyway. This is fine as long as the director requires nothing complicated. Of course, if the bows are to be choreographed over music, then they will need to be thought-out well in advance, and preferably rehearsed at an earlier stage.

Everyone will have a different approach to curtain calls, and it very much depends upon the taste of the director as to how these will be handled. Personally I tend to avoid long, drawn-out curtain calls, which can often seem self-satisfied and indulgent. In most cases I also try to acknowledge the company of actors rather than the individuals, although this obviously depends upon the type of musical being presented. *Hair* and *Godspell*, for example, are shows which are pretty much ensemble pieces, and I believe that in such cases all the performers should be acknowledged together. However, it would seem strange to the audience, I think, if a production of *My Fair Lady*, or *Hello, Dolly!* failed to single out their leading actors.

12 · The first night and beyond

The opening night

Even though the actors will probably be fairly preoccupied just before the show, it is important, I think, for the director (and perhaps the choreographer and producer too) to go round the dressing rooms and wish everybody luck. It is also important to remember that the stage managers will probably be feeling just as anxious as the actors, and a word of encouragement in their ears will usually be much appreciated.

Once these courtesy calls have been made, the members of the creative team can take their places in the auditorium (with the exception of the musical director who will usually be conducting the show). Although I am a compulsive note-taker by nature, I make it a point never to take notes at the opening night performance. I try to imagine myself to be a normal member of the public, and try to see the show through the eyes of the audience (not an easy task, of course). I often experience a strange feeling of relief at this stage. Rather than feeling anxious about the performance, I tend to experience a slight feeling of detachment, which perhaps comes from the knowledge that there is very little I can actually do at this point. The show is now in the hands of the cast, the stage management, the musicians, and the crew. All I can do is hope that the hard work and dedication that has gone into the project from everyone involved will finally pay off.

The party

Reaching the end of the first night is a great cause for celebration, especially if the show has gone well and the audience has clearly had a good time. Traditionally the producer throws a party after the opening performance as a way of thanking the company for their work during the preceding weeks. Cast parties come in all shapes and sizes, and are, of course, largely dependent upon the generosity of the producer, and the size of the production budget. However limited the resources, the cast party is a very good morale booster, and allows the company members to let their hair down and celebrate the great achievement of getting the show up and running. With shows which are limited to a run of only

124

one or two weeks, the producer may decide to give a party on the last night instead of the first; the advantage here, of course, is that no one has to perform the following day.

It may seem an obvious point to make, but it is vitally important that the producer remembers to invite everyone involved in the production to the party. I have experienced too many situations where a divisive atmosphere has been created by a producer forgetting to invite members of the crew or the wardrobe department to the first night party. Since the key to a successful production is teamwork, an oversight of this nature can have a really negative effect on the company, and can make certain people feel very undervalued and excluded.

Maintaining the show

Once the first night has come and gone, the production team will need to make sure that the quality of the show remains undiminished. This means that the stage manager will need to keep a close eye on the state of the set, the props, and (in many cases) the lighting too. Depending on the length of the run, props may need to be touched up, mended, or even replaced, and the stage manager is most likely to be responsible for this. Likewise, the set may require some maintenance, and the stage manager may need to call in the designer to supervise some repainting. While the scenic and technical elements of the show are maintained by the stage manager, it is just as important to look after the quality of singing, dancing, and acting. The musical elements are fairly easy to monitor, since the musical director is normally conducting the show and is therefore aware of any changes that occur, or any laziness that may creep in on the part of the performers or the musicians in the band. A few well-judged words, and the odd clean-up rehearsal is usually enough to sort these problems out.

As far as the choreography is concerned, the choreographer should appoint a dance captain (see Chapter 9) who will keep an eye on things from within the company. In addition, the choreographer, or an assistant, should check the show at regular intervals to see that the quality of dancing is maintained. The director will also need to return to watch the show on a regular basis, not only to monitor the state of acting, but to cast a more general eye over the production as a whole. It is amazing how easily a show can deteriorate if nobody looks after it, and just as a beautiful, well-ordered garden requires tending or the inevitable result is disorder and confusion, the same could be said of a musical.

Of course, the performances will change; this is inevitable, especially where long runs are concerned. Actors are not automatons, and cannot simply repeat the same performance night after night. And even if they could, this would hardly be desirable, and would certainly be extremely uninteresting in creative terms. The actors should be allowed to develop their characters and make new discoveries, but within reason. Too much freedom can lead to unruly performances, and a general lack of focus. This is where the director needs to step in from time to time, just to advise an actor that a certain movement is too forced, or too subtle, and more generally to help maintain the clarity of the story-telling. Regular note sessions can help to iron out these sorts of on-going problems, and will also provide the actors with the comfortable feeling that the show is being well cared for. Occasionally the director may also decide to call a rehearsal in order to tighten up a specific area of the show, and to help remotivate the performers.

When taking notes on the show, it is a good idea for the director to try sitting in various parts of the auditorium. Not only will this provide the opportunity to check sight-lines, but it will also enable the director to check the sound quality, which can vary enormously depending on where a person is sitting. If there is a problem, he or she can then try to solve it by discussing it with the sound designer, or by making the actors aware that at certain points in the show they will need to work harder on their projection.

Finally, on the subject of note giving, in my experience it is often difficult to find an appropriate time to give the performers their notes. It is best to make a point of scheduling a note session into the timetable, rather than trying to catch the performers just before they go on stage. I try to avoid giving notes after the half (although sometimes it's unavoidable), and I never give notes during the show or in the interval. Most actors need time to focus their minds before going on stage, and will not appreciate any last minute words of wisdom from their director.

Warm-ups

Warm-ups will depend entirely upon the nature of the show being performed, and the type of personnel involved in the project. If the show contains a lot of dancing, it may be a good idea for the dance captain to take a physical warm-up before the show. With most professional shows the dance warm-up tends to be voluntary, since the performers are not obliged to work for more than a certain number of hours per week. The same is true of vocal warm-ups, although in my experience, most actors are grateful for the chance to get together before the performance to run through a few vocal exercises and to tighten up the odd bit of harmony from the show.

Show reports

Once the show is up and running, the stage management will need to monitor its progress, and this is usually done in the show report. This report is simply a record of day-to-day details written up after each performance, and should include timings for each act, length of interval, and audience numbers. It should also contain information concerning any absentees, both on the performing and the stage management side, and should specify any understudies who have appeared in that particular performance. The show report should also provide details concerning anything unusual that occurred during the performance, such as any technical errors, any missed entrances, and any lines of dialogue which were skipped or wrongly delivered. Once the show report has been written up, a copy should be sent to the producer so that he or she can be kept up-to-date with the progress of the show. In addition to the show report, there should also be an accident book which describes in detail any accident sustained by a member of the cast, stage management or crew, which is in any way linked to the running of the show.

A final word

Staging a musical production requires an enormous amount of work from a dedicated team; but when everything goes well, the results can be astonishing. My fascination with musical theatre has really evolved over the last decade through working on some wonderful projects, and by coming into contact with all sorts of creative people, from directors and designers, to musicians, choreographers and, of course, actors. Not every production, naturally, has been easy, and sometimes the end result has seemed strangely at odds with the effort involved in putting the show together. But in the great majority of cases the process of putting the show on its feet has been challenging and exciting.

Nobody, of course, can guarantee the success of a musical theatre production. However, the complicated process of staging a show can certainly be facilitated by placing an emphasis upon three key elements; preparation, communication and, above all, teamwork.

Appendix

Licensing Organizations for Selected Musicals

Allegro Rodgers and Hammerstein

Anne of Green Gables Dramatic Publishing

Annie Music Theatre International

Annie Get Your Gun Rodgers and Hammerstein

Annie Warbucks Music Theatre International

Anyone Can Whistle Music Theatre International

Anything Goes Tams-Witmark

Applause Tams-Witmark

Apple Tree Music Theatre International

Archy and Mehitabel Music Theatre International

Assassins Music Theatre International

Baby Music Theatre International

Baker Street Tams-Witmark

The Baker's Wife Music Theatre International

Barnum Tams-Witmark

The Beggar's Opera Samuel French, Inc.

Bells Are Ringing Tams-Witmark

The Best Little Whorehouse in Texas Samuel French, Inc.

Big River Rodgers and Hammerstein

The Boy Friend Music Theatre International

The Boys From Syracuse Rodgers and Hammerstein

Brigadoon Tams-Witmark

Bugsy Malone Music Theatre International

By Jupiter Rodgers and Hammerstein

Cabaret Tams-Witmark

Calamity Jane Tams-Witmark

Call Me Madam Rodgers and Hammerstein

Camelot Tams-Witmark

Can-Can Tams-Witmark

Candide (Broadway) Music Theatre International

A Cantata For Anne Frank Rodgers and Hammerstein

Canterbury Tales Music Theatre International

Carnival! Tams-Witmark

Carousel Rodgers and Hammerstein

Celebration Music Theatre International and Samuel French, Inc.

Chess Samuel French, Inc.

Chicago Samuel French, Inc.

Children of Eden Music Theatre International

A Chorus Line Tams-Witmark

Christmas Carol (Legrand) Rodgers and Hammerstein

Christmas Carol (Bedloe) Samuel French, Inc.

City of Angels Tams-Witmark

Closer Than Ever Music Theatre International

The Cocoanuts Rodgers and Hammerstein

Collette Collage Music Theatre International

Company Music Theatre International

Crazy for You Tams-Witmark

Dames at Sea Samuel French, Inc.

Damn Yankees Music Theatre International

Destry Rides Again Tams-Witmark

Divorce Me, Darling! Music Theatre International

Do I Hear A Waltz? Rodgers and Hammerstein

Dr. Selavy's Magic Theatre Rodgers and
   Hammerstein
Downriver Music Theatre International
Dreams from a Summer House Samuel
   French, Inc.
The Drunkard Music Theatre International
*Elegies for Angels, Punks, and Raging
   Queens* Samuel French, Inc.
Ernest In Love Music Theatre International
Fade Out—Fade In Tams-Witmark
Fame—The Musical Music Theatre
   International
The Fantasticks Music Theatre
   International
The Farndale Mikado Samuel French, Inc.
Fawkes—the Quiet Guy Samuel French, Inc.
Fiddler on the Roof Music Theatre
   International
Finian's Rainbow Tams-Witmark
First Impressions Samuel French, Inc.
First Time Samuel French, Inc.
Flower Dream Song Rodgers and
   Hammerstein
Floyd Collins Rodgers and Hammerstein
Follies Music Theatre International
Footprints On The Moon Music Theatre
   International
Forever Plaid Music Theatre International
Forty-Second Street Tams-Witmark
Free To Be...You and Me Rodgers and
   Hammerstein
Freedom Train Music Theatre International
Frogs Dramatic Publishing
Funny Girl Tams-Witmark
*A Funny Thing Happened on the Way to the
   Forum* Music Theatre International
Game of Love Music Theatre International
Gentlemen Prefer Blondes Tams-Witmark
George M! (Yankee Doodle Dandy) Tams-
   Witmark
Gigi Tams-Witmark
The Goodbye Girl Music Theatre
   International
Good News Tams-Witmark
The Grand Tour Samuel French, Inc.
Grease Samuel French, Inc.
The Great American Backstage Musical
   Samuel French, Inc.

Great Expectations Dramatic Publishing
The Great Waltz Tams-Witmark
Guys and Dolls Music Theatre
   International
Gypsy Tams-Witmark
Hair Tams-Witmark
Half A Sixpence Dramatic Publishing
Hans Andersen Music Theatre
   International
Heidi Dramatic Publishing
Hello, Dolly! Tams-Witmark
High Button Shoes Tams-Witmark
The Hired Man Samuel French, Inc.
Hit The Deck Tams-Witmark
*How to Succeed in Business Without Really
   Trying* Music Theatre International
I'd Rather Be Right Rodgers and
   Hammerstein
I Do! I Do! Music Theatre International
I Married An Angel Rodgers and
   Hammerstein
*I'm Getting My Act Together and Taking it on
   the Road* Samuel French, Inc.
Into The Woods Music Theatre
   International
I Remember Mama Rodgers and
   Hammerstein
Irene Tams-Witmark
Irma la Douce Tams-Witmark
Jack the Ripper Samuel French, Inc.
Jane Eyre Dramatic Publishing
Jesus Christ, Superstar Music Theatre
   International
Joseph & the Amazing Technicolor Dreamcoat
   Music Theatre International
The King and I Rodgers and Hammerstein
Kiss Me, Kate Tams-Witmark
Kiss of the Spiderwoman Samuel French,
   Inc.
Knickerbocker Holiday Rodgers and
   Hammerstein
La Cage Aux Folles Samuel French, Inc.
Lady, Be Good! Tams-Witmark
Lady Audley's Secret Music Theatre
   International
Lady In the Dark Rodgers and
   Hammerstein
Leave It To Jane Tams-Witmark

Let 'Em Eat Cake Music Theatre International

Li'l Abner Tams-Witmark

Little Mary Sunshine Samuel French, Inc.

Little Me Tams-Witmark

A Little Night Music Music Theatre International

Little Shop of Horrors Music Theatre International

Lost In the Stars Rodgers and Hammerstein

Louisiana Purchase Rodgers and Hammerstein

Love From Judy Samuel French, Inc.

Lucky Stiff Music Theatre International

Lust Samuel French, Inc.

Mack and Mabel Samuel French, Inc.

Mame Tams-Witmark

Man of La Mancha Tams-Witmark

Me and Juliet Rodgers and Hammerstein

Me and My Girl Samuel French, Inc.

Meet Me in St. Louis Tams-Witmark

The Middle of Nowhere (Newman) Rodgers and Hammerstein

Miss Liberty Rodgers and Hammerstein

Mister President Rodgers and Hammerstein

The Most Happy Fella Music Theatre International

The Music Man Music Theatre International

My Fair Lady Tams-Witmark

My Favorite Year Music Theatre International

My One and Only Tams-Witmark

Naughty Marietta Tams-Witmark

The New Moon Tams-Witmark

Nine Samuel French, Inc.

No, No, Nanette (1971 Only) Tams-Witmark

No Strings Rodgers and Hammerstein

Nunsense Samuel French, Inc.

Nunsense II Tams-Witmark

Oh, Brother! Samuel French, Inc.

Oh, Captain! Tams-Witmark

Oh, Kay! Tams-Witmark

Oil City Symphony Music Theatre International

Oklahoma! Rodgers and Hammerstein

Oliver! Tams-Witmark

On The Town Tams-Witmark

On The Twentieth Century Samuel French, Inc.

On Your Toes Rodgers and Hammerstein

Once Upon A Mattress Rodgers and Hammerstein

One Touch Of Venus Rodgers and Hammerstein

Orpheus In the Underworld Samuel French, Inc.

Pacific Overtures Music Theatre International

Paint Your Wagon Tams-Witmark

The Pajama Game Music Theatre International

Pal Joey Rodgers and Hammerstein

Passion Music Theatre International

Peter Pan (Chater-Robinson) Samuel French, Inc.

Phantom of the Country Opera Music Theatre International

Phantom of the Opera (Ken Hill) Samuel French, Inc.

Philomen Music Theatre International

Pinocchio (M. Rogers) Rodgers and Hammerstein

Pipe Dream Rodgers and Hammerstein

Pippin Music Theatre International

Promises, Promises Tams-Witmark

Pump Boys and Dinettes Samuel French, Inc.

Rags Rodgers and Hammerstein

The Red Mill Tams-Witmark

Return to the Forbidden Planet Samuel French, Inc.

The Rink Samuel French, Inc.

Riverwind Music Theatre International

The Roar of the Greasepaint—The Smell of the Crowd Tams-Witmark

The Robber Bridegroom Music Theatre International

Robert and Elizabeth Samuel French, Inc.

Rock Nativity Music Theatre International

Rose-Marie Tams-Witmark

Salad Days Tams-Witmark

Salvation Music Theatre International

The Secret Life of Walter Mitty Samuel French, Inc.
Seesaw Samuel French, Inc.
Seven Brides For Seven Brothers Music Theatre International
She Loves Me Music Theatre International
Show Boat Rodgers and Hammerstein
Singin' In The Rain Music Theatre International
Six Women with Brain Death or *Expiring Minds Want to Know* Music Theatre International
A Slice of Saturday Night Samuel French, Inc.
Smokey Joe's Café Rodgers and Hammerstein
Some Canterbury Tales Samuel French, Inc.
Something's Afoot Samuel French, Inc.
Snoopy!!! Tams-Witmark
Songbook Samuel French, Inc.
Song and Dance Rodgers and Hammerstein
Song of Norway Tams-Witmark
The Sound of Music Rodgers and Hammerstein
South Pacific Rodgers and Hammerstein
State Fair Rodgers and Hammerstein
The Stingiest Man in Town Music Theatre International
Stop the World—I Want To Get Off Tams-Witmark
Street Scene Rodgers and Hammerstein
Strider Samuel French, Inc.
Strike Up the Band Music Theatre International
The Student Prince Tams-Witmark
Sugar (Some Like It Hot) Tams-Witmark
Summer Stock Murder Rodgers and Hammerstein
Sunday In the Park With George Music Theatre International
Sunny Tams-Witmark
Sweeney Todd Music Theatre International
Sweet Adeline Rodgers and Hammerstein
Sweet Charity Tams-Witmark
Sweethearts Tams-Witmark
Teddy and Alice Music Theatre International

Teller of Tales Samuel French, Inc.
They're Playing Our Song Samuel French, Inc.
The Threepenny Opera Rodgers and Hammerstein
The Tin Pan Alley Rag (Berlin/Joplin) Rodgers and Hammerstein
Treasure Island (Ornadel) Music Theatre International
Two By Two Rodgers and Hammerstein
Two Gentlemen of Verona Tams-Witmark
The Unsinkable Molly Brown Music Theatre International
The Vagabond King Tams-Witmark
Very Warm for May Rodgers and Hammerstein
Viva, Mexico Samuel French, Inc.
Walking Happy Samuel French, Inc.
Western Star Music Theatre International
West Side Story Music Theatre International
What About Luv? Music Theatre International
Where's Charley? Music Theatre International
Whistle Down the Wind (Taylor) Rodgers and Hammerstein
White Horse Inn Samuel French, Inc.
Wild, Wild Women Samuel French, Inc.
Wildcat on Safari Music Theatre International
The Will Rogers Follies Tams-Witmark
Wind in the Willows (Perry) Rodgers and Hammerstein
Wings Rodgers and Hammerstein
The Wiz Samuel French, Inc.
The Wizard of Oz (Two Versions: MGM/RSC) Tams-Witmark
A Wonderful Life (Rafoso) Rodgers and Hammerstein
Wonderful Town Tams-Witmark
Working Music Theatre International
Your Own Thing Tams-Witmark
You're A Good Man, Charlie Brown Tams-Witmark
Yours, Anne Rodgers and Hammerstein

Compilation Shows

Ain't Misbehavin' (Fats Waller) Music Theatre International
All Kinds of People (Hammerstein) Rodgers and Hammerstein
The All Night Strut Music Theatre International
Berlin to Broadway with Kurt Weill Music Theatre International
Blues In the Night Music Theatre International
Closer Than Ever (Shire) Music Theatre International
Cole Samuel French, Inc.
Cowardy Custard (Noel Coward) Samuel French, Inc.
Decline and Fall of the Entire World As Seen Through the Eyes of Cole Porter Rodgers and Hammerstein
Eubie! (Eubie Blake) Music Theatre International
A Grand Night For Singing Rodgers and Hammerstein
I Love You, You're Perfect, Now Change Rodgers and Hammerstein
Jacques Brel Is Alive and Well and Living in Paris Music Theatre International
Lies and Legends (Chapin) Rodgers and Hammerstein
Marry Me A Little (Sondheim) Music Theatre International
The Melody Lingers On (Berlin) Rodgers and Hammerstein
Noel and Gertie (Coward) Samuel French, Inc.
No Frills Revue (Marvin Hamlisch, etc.) Music Theatre International
Red Hot and Cole Music Theatre International
Side by Side By Sondheim Music Theatre International
Sing For Your Supper (Rodgers and Hart) Rodgers and Hammerstein

Some Enchanted Evening (R & H) Rodgers and Hammerstein
Sophisticated Ladies (Duke Ellington) Rodgers and Hammerstein
Starting Here, Starting Now (Shire) Music Theatre International
When the Cookie Crumbles You Can Still Pick Up the Pieces Music Theatre International
You're Gonna Love Tomorrow Music Theatre International

Addresses of Licensing Organizations:

Dramatic Publishing
PO Box 129
Woodstock, IL 60098-0129
(800) 448-7469

Music Theatre International
421 West 54th Street
New York, NY 10019
(212) 541-4684

Rodgers & Hammerstein Theatre Library
1065 Avenue of the Americas
Suite 2400
New York, NY 10018
(212) 541-6600

Samuel French Ltd.
45 West 25th Street
New York, NY 10010
(212) 206-8990

Tams-Witmark Music Library Inc. (Musicscope)
560 Lexington Avenue
New York, NY 10022
(212) 688-2525

Bookstores Specializing in Musical Theater

The Drama Book Shop
723 7th Avenue
New York, NY 10019
(212) 944-0595

Applause Bookstore
211 West 71st Street
New York, NY 10023
(212) 595-4735
applause@buybroadway.com

Drama Books
134 9th Street
San Francisco, CA 94103
(415) 255-0604

Further Reading

The ABC of Stage Technology, Frances Reid (Heinemann)
Choosing and Staging a Play, Guy Williams (Players Press)
Designing for the Theatre, Frances Reid (Routledge)
Directors in Rehearsal, Susan Letzler Cole (Routledge)
Games for Actors and Non-Actors, Augusto Boal (Routledge)
How to Direct a Musical, Daniel Young (Routledge)
The Musical From Inside Out, Stephen Citron (Ivan R. Dee, Inc.)
Performing in Musicals, Elaine Adams Novak (Schirmer)
Scene Design and Stage Lighting, W. Oren Parker & R. Craig Wolf (Holt, Rinehart, Winston)
The Show Makers, Lawrence Thelen (Routledge)
Sound for the Theatre, Graham Walne (Routledge)
Stage Lighting for Theatre Designers, Nigel H. Morgan (Heinemann)
The Stage Lighting Handbook, Frances Reid (Routledge)
Stage Make-up: Step by Step, Rosemarie Swinfield (Betterway Publications)
Stage Management: A Gentle Art, Daniel Bond (Routledge)
Staging Dance, Susan Cooper (Routledge)
Staging Musical Theatre, Elaine and Deborah Novak (Betterway Publications)

Index